GOOD HOUSEKEEPING
FAMILY LIBRARY

HANDBOOK OF EASY GARDEN PLANTS

GOOD HOUSEKEEPING
FAMILY LIBRARY
HANDBOOK OF
EASY GARDEN
PLANTS

Sheila Howarth

SPHERE BOOKS LIMITED
30–32 Grays Inn Road, London, WC1X 8JL

First published in Great Britain in 1974 by
Ebury Press
First Sphere Books edition 1976

ISBN 0 7221 3957 8

Cover picture: John Cowley

Printed and bound in Great Britain by
Cox & Wyman Ltd, London, Fakenham and Reading

CONTENTS

1 GUIDELINES FOR THE EASY GARDEN

What one person does with ease, another does with difficulty – or not at all. The same applies to plants, and for much the same reasons. They must have the natural ability to succeed, plus the right environment and plenty of encouragement. Plants can be just as variable as people, thriving in one garden, failing next door, even when treatment and soil may have been identical.

In selecting the plants described in this book, I have stressed the need to understand their individual requirements. There is always a temptation to buy on impulse when one sees an attractive plant flowering in its container at a garden centre. You take it home, often unaware of the size to which it will eventually grow, or what it likes in the way of soil and situation. No acid soil lover is 'easy' in alkaline surroundings, and *vice versa*. So, for a start, let us save money, time and effort, by taking the trouble to find out whether the plant we admire so much will, in fact, thrive in our particular surroundings. Never be afraid to ask for advice from your garden centre or seedsman; do not hesitate to pry into nearby gardens, and sooner, rather than later, you will achieve the success you deserve.

What do we mean by easy plants, anyway? The answer is those that require no special soil or site; no staking or deadheading, with an ability to survive drought and, when in flower, have blooms that neither rain nor frost will ruin. Easier still are those shrubs, trees, bulbs and perennials which, once planted, look after themselves without undue nannying, need no transplanting, thinning, or rigid pruning. In short,

7

plants that may almost outlive whoever planted them. Easy annuals must stand the rigid test of not needing any support. They must be weatherproof; willing to be raised from seed without heat and die without fuss. Some annuals are welcome because they behave in this way, but they must be chosen with care, so that the seedlings stay in the area you have given them and do not stray on to lawns or rose beds. Other possibilities are self-climbing plants; evergreen ground cover, and hedges that need no clipping.

The word easy also implies freedom from restraint, and certainly, the easiest plants of all to grow are those that take to you so willingly that they could become an eventual embarrassment – plants such as Chinese lanterns or the Russian vine, which can take over the garden if given half a chance.

Let's start with some general definitions and advice on managing the various groups of plants – annuals, perennials and so on that you will want to include in your garden.

Annuals

An annual is a plant which grows from seed and completes its life cycle in twelve months or less. It flowers, produces seed, then dies, and consequently must be sown every year. It is the cheapest way of having a mass of brilliant blooms. The colours are particularly bright because they have to attract insects quickly for fertilization. Their life is so short they are in a hurry to produce seed.

They are usually sown from March till June, directly into the open ground where they are to flower. Those to be used entirely as cut flowers for the house can be grown in short rows in any odd part of the garden which does not expect admiration, but gets some sun. This could perhaps be among the vegetables.

Annuals should be looked on as heart-warming summer visitors; here today, gone by autumn . . . leaving no recriminations. Gay guests, full of smiles and making few demands . . . certainly not a feather bed. But whatever quarters you provide them with, never let there be overcrowding or there will be deaths from suffocation.

8

Preparing the soil

The ground should be prepared by digging in autumn, winter or early spring, the earlier the better so that wind and frost can do their work of breaking down the clumps. If there are no perennial weeds to be removed there is no need to fork over the surface deeper than 6 in.

Soils which are in good heart need no manure, but those in poor shape and condition should have well-rotted compost or manure dug into the surface. This improves the structure as well as adding nourishment. Heavy soils will rake down later to a better consistency if sedge peat is forked into the surface at the rate of a bucketful to the sq yd.

In spring when the soil begins to warm, rake down the bed to the fine tilth needed for small seeds to germinate. The texture should be that of caster sugar, rather than rice. Give a second shallow forking and raking at least two weeks before you start sowing the seeds so that the ground can settle. Then tread the surface firmly to make sure there are no nooks, crannies or air pockets for the seeds to fall into and prevent germination. Never do this unless the soil is quite dry. When it is sticky, keep off or you will make mud patches in which nothing would ever germinate. Seeds sown late in good conditions will catch up and do better than those sown earlier in poor ones.

Sowing

The depth at which the seed is sown depends on its size . . . it needs a covering to match. Large seeds like lupins and nasturtiums can be sown almost an inch deep, but fine ones such as godetia need only a sprinkle of soil over them, or their shoots would never struggle through to the light.

Sow the seeds very thinly, either broadcast or in drills (very shallow grooves). These can be made with a draw hoe, or (I find more evenly) by laying the handle of the hoe on the surface and pressing it in to the required depth. The soil must be kept moist until the seedlings appear.

When they are an inch or so high, thin them to a few inches apart. A second and final thinning should leave the plants so that they are three-quarters of their final height from each other. Keep them free of weeds.

9

The thinnings of many varieties can be transplanted to other parts of the garden when they are still small. Choose a dull day during showery weather so that the roots will be moist and the foliage will not get shrivelled in hot sun.

If the seeds are to broadcast directly where they are to grow in the border, rake and firm the·soil, then with a stick mark out drifts of irregular sizes and shapes where the different varieties are to go. Another method is to edge the boundaries with a trickle of sand.

Make sure not to get a dwarf type trapped in the middle of tall ones, or it will not get enough light and sun. Label the patches with name and height, so you know how far apart to thin them.

Sowing thinly is a knack which does not come easily to everyone. Those inclined to be ham-fisted at this delicate operation should mix the seed with four times the amount of sand.

Many hardy annuals can be sown outside in August and September to provide flowers early the following year.

Never allow the dead flowers to go to seed. By taking off the faded blooms you can keep the plants flowering throughout the summer.

Half-hardy annuals

There is no strict division between these and hardy annuals, for what may be hardy in one part of the country will not be in another. Most of the popular summer bedding plants are found in this group which includes both true half-hardy annuals and some perennials, such as antirrhinums, which are usually treated and best grown in this manner and then discarded. If left to behave as perennials the plants become straggly over the years and the blooms deteriorate.

Half-hardies must have warmer conditions in the early stages than our British gardens can offer. They are usually raised from seed sown in pots or boxes in a greenhouse, frame, or indoors from early February till the end of April.

Sowing
Many half-hardies can be sown in the open ground from the

10

end of May till early June, but their flowers will be much later and probably get damaged by frost while there are still many buds left to open.

To get seeds off to an early start, thoroughly clean whatever container you are going to use; the seeds need good drainage holes and a layer of crocks. Use a fine, porous medium such as sedge peat and sand or a no-soil compost. Press it firm, sow thinly and evenly, and, in most cases, only just cover the seeds with a thin layer of soil or silver sand. Keep the compost just moist and not too wet, using a fine rose for watering and keep them at a temperature of 55–60 °F.

When large enough to handle, prick off the seedlings into boxes, and later, gradually harden them off, by giving them more ventilation and cooler conditions, until it is safe to plant them in their flowering positions during May and June.

For the novice raising his own half-hardies, the worst hazard is the risk of the seedlings 'damping-off' at an early age, i.e., becoming attacked by disease which causes them to decay at soil level. To guard against this, sow thinly; thin them early so they do not become 'drawn'; don't let the atmosphere get damp and stuffy; water with Cheshunt compound. Pricking off at the earliest possible stage is the real secret of growing half-hardy annuals.

There are now many electrical propagating cases, if you have no greenhouse, in which the seeds can be kept at temperatures up to 70 °F until they germinate. But you must always be on the alert or they will spring up and overgrow while your back is turned. They must be pricked off when really tiny, and put somewhere cooler.

Airing cupboards and the space above (never directly on top of) central heating radiators, particularly night storage heaters, are excellent spots for germinating half-hardies – and cost nothing extra. Some seedhouses sell mini-cloches already filled with a growing compost. You sow the chosen seeds, according to the particular instructions, water, and keep them on a window-sill till they are ready for the garden.

For the home-made method, use any size of pot or seed tray which is most convenient. You could use Jiffy pots made of compressed peaty mixture, which encourages strong roots and means no transplanting. You simply plant the whole pot when the time is ripe, but avoid letting the peat dry out.

Whatever container you choose, sow very, very thinly. It avoids wasting seeds, prevents overcrowding when they germinate and means less time wasted in thinning-out later. Put the containers into sealed plastic bags and keep them in a warm, dark place till they germinate. If you have nowhere dark, cover them with paper bags.

As soon as the seedlings are up, remove the coverings, then regulate the light carefully. Seedlings need plenty of light, but they don't like to be roasted or dazzled. Keep them out of scorching sun and very bright light till they are old and sturdy enough to tackle the great outdoors. On cloudy days give them all the light that is going. As the seedlings are moved to a cooler room to be hardened off you can use your airing cupboard, or other 'hot spots' to raise another batch of seedlings.

The advantage of having the seeds right under your nose in the house is that you won't forget them and will notice at once if they are getting too leggy, or drying out, or need any kind of attention. The disadvantage is that they take up a good deal of space at a most undecorative stage in their lives.

Perennials

These are plants which flower each year and live for an indefinite period. Many of them can be raised easily from seed sown outdoors in late spring and summer. Seedling perennials, as a general rule, are more vigorous than plants propagated by means of divisions and cuttings.

Preparing the soil
Make a fairly rich seed bed in a sheltered and sunny position. If the ground is heavy fork dry sedge peat into the top 2 in at the rate of a bucketful to the sq yd. Where the soil is sandy and dry, damp the peat well before using it. Make the bed really firm by treading and follow this by a light raking.

Sowing
Sow the seed thinly in drills. These should be watered first if

the ground is dry. No further watering is usually necessary unless there is a long dry spell when the plants are tiny, as the roots will be too small to go deeper and find damper soil.

Keep free from weeds and pests and when large enough to handle, transplant them carefully to a nursery bed. They can be moved to their permanent homes in October or early spring. This will depend on the size of the plants and on soil and weather conditions. On heavy soils it is often better to wait till spring so that the young plants do not run the risk of dying in a cold, wet spot before they are old enough to look after themselves.

Unless you want a great number of plants, the nursery bed can be skipped altogether, provided the seedlings are well thinned out early in life so that they make sturdy plants.

Many perennials and biennials flower well the first year if they are sown early under glass and given the same treatment as for half-hardy annuals.

Growing permanent plants from seed is a tremendous economy as well as excitement for the beginner with a lot of empty space to fill and little experience of growing anything. But for the latest named varieties of hardy perennials which can only be obtained from cuttings or divisions you will have to go to a specialist nursery and pay specialist prices. Although the initial outlay will be much more expensive, if there is a particular variety you simply must have, then buy it – at least three plants of a kind – and in a few years you should be able to divide and increase your original investment, and discard more ordinary varieties you have grown from seed.

The mixed or herbaceous border
The hardy perennial is a permanent resident of a mixed or herbaceous border. The herbaceous ones are those which lose their foliage in autumn and retreat out of sight till spring after the dead stems have been cut to the ground. In cold northern areas the stems can be left until spring to help protect the roots from frost and cold winds.

It is also a good idea to leave a few dead stems of any clumps which you intend to split up and transplant in spring, so you can recognize where they are when the time comes, which is

13

usually before they have sent up any recognizable new shoots.

The standard advice for a herbaceous border is that it should be dug over every three years, fed with compost or manure and the plants divided, discarding old dead centres of clumps and replanting the new outer pieces. Today, however, this can be taken with a pinch of salt, as not many true herbaceous borders exist. Few of us have the space or inclination to leave even a small bed with nothing to see but soil for the whole winter.

They have been replaced with mixed borders of hardy perennials, which include many evergreens and evergreys of different heights and habit. Many of these would be most distressed if the three-year turnover cycle (programme) came within sniffing distance of their roots, or they would refuse to flower the following year, or even more.

Notorious resenters of disturbance are paeonies, hellebores, hemerocallis (day lilies): kniphofia (red-hot poker); hosta (plaintain lilies) and alstroemeria (Peruvian lily).

Planning a hardy perennial border

The purpose of such a border or island bed is to give colour in the form of flowers or foliage for as long a period as possible. The ideal situation is a southern aspect, light and airy with no drip from trees, some shelter from the most evil prevailing winds, and a good well-drained soil. This, though, is perfection and the plants in this book will settle for a good deal less, unless a special warning is given.

Try and plan the plantings so that as one clump of flowers fades and dies down, neighbours are coming up on all sides to disguise the fact.

Never have single plants dotted about as on fabric patterns. In the growing world you need generous drifts and clumps of irregular sizes and shapes.

Be careful to vary the heights as well as leaf shape and shade. Use the spiky ones among the softer bushy growers, to draw attention to their differences.

Most important of all is to harmonize the colours. Avoid a 'twopence coloured' effect at all costs, or regimented stations of red, white and blue. This means keeping a careful eye on

14

flowering times so that something of shocking pink has expired before a flame coloured something else is in competition. Mauves and pinks hate to be beside anything with bronze foliage, and when you are at a loss to prevent a quarrel and transplanting is not feasible, put in a quick-growing silvered foliage plant as a peacemaker.

Biennials

The cultural treatment of biennials is almost the same as that of hardy perennials, but they are of very little use after one flowering season. Or you can consider them as annuals which take two years to accomplish what they do in one. They germinate from seed the first year, bloom through the second . . . and then goodbye. As already mentioned, many attractive perennials are better treated as biennials since their performance 'goes off' in subsequent years. Among these are sweet William, hollyhock, wallflower and antirrhinum. With the help of small propagators and new methods, the dividing lines between permanent and throw-away plants is a stamen wide.

2 A SELECTION OF TROUBLE-FREE PLANTS

Annuals

ALYSSUM Popular plants for dwarf edgings, formal bedding and in paving crevices. From 4–6 in. White, pink, purple and a new yellow introduction called *saxatile compactum*, 'Goldball'. Seed can be sown in April to flower June to October, or in autumn for early flowers.

CALENDULA (marigold or pot marigold) Foolproof and will grow in poor soil. Good for cutting. Yellow, orange, apricot, cream, from 10 in–2 ft. Sow from March to May according to weather and district. (See opposite.)

CANDYTUFT Easy and quick-growing, white, pink, crimson-carmine and shades of mauve and purple. 8–15 in, compact and will grow in almost any soil or situation.

CHRYSANTHEMUM Single daisy-like flowers with coloured rings in brilliant shades. $1-2\frac{1}{2}$ ft. Very showy, they flower over a long period. Excellent for borders and cutting. Sow in April where they are to grow and thin out from $1-1\frac{1}{2}$ ft apart.

CLARKIA One of the easiest annuals, white, pink and red, 1–2 ft. Plant in small groups for best effect.

CLARY (*Salvia horminum*) Highly-coloured leaves or bracts in 'arty' shades of pink, rose, white, blue and purple, which retain their colour for several months. $1\frac{1}{2}-2$ ft. Excellent for

16   Pot marigold (*Calendula officinalis* 'Orange King Improved'). *See above.*

indoor decoration and can be dried for winter flower arrangements.

CORNFLOWER Grows well in any soil in a sunny situation. Good as cut flowers. There are both dwarf and tall varieties, 15 in to 3 ft, in shades of blue, rose, maroon, white and lavender. Sow from March onwards and thin out to 9–12 in apart.

ESCHSCHOLTZIA (Californian poppy) Brilliant semi-double and frilled flowers in shades of red, orange, yellow, white as well as subtle and unusual shades. Easy going even on poor dry soil but must have sun. Sow where they are to flower in March or April and thin to 8 in apart. 1 ft high. (See page 21.)

GODETIA Easy and long-lasting plants which have much in common with the clarkias. Large and vivid flowers of dwarf and tall varieties from 6 in–2½ ft in many shades. Sow in March or April where they are to grow and thin ruthlessly. Seedlings *don't* take kindly to being transplanted. (See page 24.)

GYPSOPHILA (cloud plant: baby's breath) White and rose pink, 1½ ft. Likes chalk and good drainage but will do well on other soils which are not heavy and soggy. Sow from March to July.

HELICHRYSUM The most popular of everlasting flowers and obvious long-lasters in borders and beds. Stiff, paper-like double-daisy flowers in shades of rose, crimson, orange, white, and art shades. The dwarf strain is 1½ ft and the tall one, 3 ft.

LARKSPUR Good for cutting, white, blue, scarlet, salmon, lilac. Heights and shapes to suit all gardens. The double dwarf hyacinth-flowered is only 1 ft high, while the 'Giant Imperial' reaches 4 ft, branches out from the base and produces double flowers. They love sun and hate to be transplanted. Sow where they are to flower in autumn and spring and thin well.

LAVATERA (mallow) White and pink trumpet-shaped flowers 3–4 in across. Bushy plants for the back of borders, 3 ft tall. Sow in the open in April. The flowers form in masses from early August till autumn.

LINARIA (toadflax) Pretty little antirrhinum-like flower in many beautiful colours, 8 in to 1 ft. Fine for edgings and bedding.

LINUM (flax) White, blue, pink or scarlet, extremely free-flowering and does well in poor soil if it is sunny. Sow in April where they are to flower. There are several types, *L. grandiflorum* which grows to 2 ft and more, to the scarlet flax of 1 ft which needs bold groups for full effect.

LOVE-LIES-BLEEDING (amaranthus) Grows to a height of 2–3 ft, with strange drooping, sometimes furry, tassels of crimson or green. Sow April or May where they are to flower.

LUPINUS (annual lupin) An unusual and effective plant which deserves to be better known. It flourishes in most soils. There is a 'Pixie' strain with gay shades of pink, rose, blue and lavender together with white and bi-coloured varieties, only 1 ft high. Others grow to 3 ft. Sow in April where they are to flower.

MALOPE An old-fashioned splendid border plant, good for cutting, 2–3½ ft with large trumpet-shaped flowers of carmine-red, rose, crimson and white, on firm stems. Sow in late April in rich soil and a sunny position. (See page 25.)

NASTURTIUM Succeeds specially well on poor, sandy soil. 9–12 in. Unusual and new varieties: 'Alaska', dwarf and compact with variegated leaves of green and cream with the flowers well above in shades of crimson, yellow, orange, salmon and cerise. 'Whirlbird Scarlet', unique in that the flowers are without the usual back spur, and consequently sit open-faced, right on top of the stems and well above the foliage, creating a blaze of fiery orange-scarlet flowers.

PHACELIA The best known and loved is *P. campanularia*, 9 in high, with brilliant gentian-blue bell-shaped flowers and grey-ish-green leaves tinged with red. *P. c.* 'Blue Bonnet' is 1½ ft with equally intense blue flowers; it needs a sunny position and flowers in 6–8 weeks after sowing. *P. tanacetifolia* (wild heliotrope) has curled flower heads which unfurl into clusters of lavender-blue flowers, $1\frac{1}{2}$–2 ft. The plants are favourites with bees.

POPPY These can always be relied upon to produce a feast for the eye with the minimum of effort. White, pink, red and delicate bi-colour. Paeony-flowered and Shirley strain, 18–24 in. Sow March or April where they are to flower, as seedlings refuse to be transplanted.

SUNFLOWER (helianthus) Apart from the 6–10 ft giants with yellow flowers, there are more companionable varieties. 'Dwarf Sungold' is $2\frac{1}{2}$ ft with large, intensely double flowers of golden yellow on small, branching plants. 'Autumn Tints' has charming medium-sized single flowers on strong stems, produced freely on very branching plants; the flowers of yellow-bronze and chestnut-red are excellent for cutting. Sow the seeds in April where they are to grow . . . in the sun, naturally.

SWEET WILLIAM 'Wee Willie', 4–6 in. A new, surprising introduction. They come into bloom when the plants are only 2 in high. The single flowers are $\frac{3}{4}$ in across in bright shades of ruby, rose-pink, crimson. Excellent for edgings. 'Dwarf Red Monarch,' 9 in, large rounded heads of bright scarlet-red. Good for bedding and cutting. 'Annual Mixed', 1 ft, produces large flower heads, zoned and having darker edges to the petals in the full colour range of the more commonly-grown biennial types.

SWEET SULTAN (*Centaurea imperialis*) 'Giant Double Mixed'. $1\frac{1}{2}$ ft, a magnificent strain with fringed, scented flowers of pink, lavender, purple, yellow, white. Easy to grow and good to cut.

VIRGINIA STOCK One of the easiest and hardiest for almost any situation. Confetti-like flowers, 6–9 in, in shades of lilac, mauve, red, yellow and white.

Eschscholzia (*E. californica* 'Mission Bells'). *See page 18.*

VISCARIA Showy, trouble-free, thrives in open sunny positions and should be more widely grown. 1 ft, in soft pastel shades of rose, blue, pink, coral, lavender.

XERANTHEMUM Pretty 'everlasting'. $1\frac{1}{2}$–2 ft, with crested, double cornflower-like blooms of white, purple, lilac and rose, carried on long stems. Lends a unique colour to winter bouquets.

Annual climbers

COBAEA *scandens* Rapid grower for a sunny wall and poor soil. Treat it too well and it will not flower. The deep violet cup-and-saucer blooms resemble those of Canterbury bells and when they first open are a sage green.

ECCREMOCARPUS *scaber* (Chilean glory vine) Very showy with sprays of bright orange-red tubular flowers and attractive ferny foliage. Generally grown as an annual, it is in fact a per-ennial. If you can protect it at ground level with straw or bracken, it may sprout afresh from the base next year, though its top will not survive the winter.

MORNING GLORY (ipomoea) One of the most striking annual climbers, with magnificent azure-blue trumpet blooms, each of which lasts only a few hours . . . from breakfast till teatime. A new crop appears next morning. Besides the original blue kinds, there are now rose and mauve ones with flowers more than 4 in across. To get a long season from them, chip the seed (by making a gash in the hard outer casing) or soak in warm water for twenty-four hours to help germination, and start them off in slight warmth in March. They like moister and richer conditions than most annual climbers. (See page 29.)

TROPAEOLUM *canariense* (canary creeper) A close relative of the nasturtium, this smothers itself with dainty fringed yellow flowers for months and grows rampantly from seed. It often drops seed on the ground below to give you plants for next season. It will scale a 12 ft trellis in one season and enjoys the same conditions as other nasturtiums – poor.

THUNBERGIA *alata* (black-eyed Susan) Only for warm and sunny positions outdoors, but excellent for verandas and balconies. Grow several plants in a large pot. White, buff and orange-coloured flowers with black centres.

Half-hardy annuals

ANTIRRHINUM A chameleon plant, it has almost lost its original identity. There are hyacinth-flowered, penstemon-flowered, pixies, dwarfs, Tom Thumbs as well as rust-resistant varieties. They come in all colours and shapes, some branching, others tall and stately, from 9 in–4 ft.

AMARANTHUS *caudatus* (love-lies-bleeding) Crimson or green. Drooping and sometimes furry tassels, $2\frac{1}{2}$ ft. Needs a warm sunny place where the soil is not too rich, such as a south-facing wall. Can also be treated as a hardy annual by sowing in April or May where plants are to flower. (See page 32.)

ARCTOTIS (African daisy) Handsome border plant and excellent for cutting, being graceful and long-stemmed. Likes soil dry and sunny. Brilliant shades of red, orange, yellow, apricot, carmine, cream and white. Many flowers have inner rings with contrasting colours. 1 ft–2 ft.

ASTERS As many shapes, shades and behaviours as you can imagine . . . giants, Lilliputs, powderpuffs, ostrich feather, quilled, totem pole, and many others. From 6 in–$2\frac{1}{2}$ ft. Can also be sown in the open in early May.

BALSAM For bedding or front of borders. Camellia-flowered, showy pink, white, salmon and scarlet flowers; $1\frac{1}{2}$ ft. 'Tom Thumb', a dwarf strain, 10 in, with large individual flowers in rosy salmon shades, cerise red, scarlet, mauve and white. 'Dwarf Spotted Mixture', an interesting new development. Several colours, all of them spotted white. The compact plants are about 15 in high and 18 in wide and come into flower two months after they are sown.

COSMOS (*cosmea*) White, pink, crimson and scarlet. Single and

(*Above*) Godetia (*G. grandiflora*) and (*opposite*) Malope (*M. trifida*).
See pages 18 and 19.

semi-double flowers from 2–5 in across, on 3–4 ft wiry stems, and fern-like foliage. Long lasting as cut flowers.

DIANTHUS (annual pinks) Succeeds anywhere which is not damp or shady. 4–15 in, long flowering and a mass of bloom, many scented and up to $2\frac{1}{2}$ in across. Very showy, for bedding, rock gardens, window-boxes, etc. (See page 33.)

NEMESIA Few flowers are capable of making such glorious bedding displays. 9–12 in. Huge colour range which look more effective in mixed colours than single ones.

NICOTIANA (tobacco plant) White, lime-green, crimson, pink, lemon, 1–3 ft, thriving in almost all soils and positions. All are sweetly scented except 'Lime-Green', which is a favourite of flower arrangers. The flowers remain fully open during the day.

PETUNIAS The best are F1 hybrids, which are always a little more expensive because their seed can only be produced by hand pollination. A vast variety to choose from 6–15 in. White, purple, mauve, blue, pink, red, bronze, coral-salmon, orange; single, double, striped and frilled. They need sun and a good summer. The Double Multiflora varieties, 12–15 in, have double frilled carnation-like blooms $2\frac{1}{2}$ in across on bushy plants; they are remarkably rainproof. They also have an exceptionally long flowering period. Many lovely shades.

PHLOX *drummondii* Blue, violet, pink, rose, salmon, scarlet, white. 6–15 in. Mostly neat, compact plants, effective in masses, many with contrasting eyes. 'Large-flowered Mixed' is good for cutting. They can also be sown outdoors from May onwards.

STOCKS (Ten-week) 100 per cent double-flowered fragrant stocks have replaced the old sorts, in which a number of single-flowered plants could not be avoided. 1–$1\frac{1}{2}$ ft. Compact and bushy or tall, single stems tightly packed with extra large florets which make them good for cutting. Shades of white, lavender, pink, blood-red and primrose.

VERBENA Will flower from July to October and thrives in wet or sunny seasons. 6–15 in. Good for cutting. Shades of lavender, pink, salmon, scarlet.

ZINNIA Giant, Lilliput, pompon forms, 1–2½ ft. Pink, orange, gold, scarlet, white, yellow, lavender. Dahlia-flowered, dwarfs with tiny heads, and dwarfs with huge heads, semi-double, and 'Sombrero' which has single flowers 2½ in across, crimson with yellow tips. Seedlings do not like disturbance and may do better sown where they are to flower in May and June.

Biennials

As already mentioned, these come in an uneasy gap between annuals and perennials. Treat them in the manner which suits you best.

They are most often used in a formal way, in front gardens, or along paths and terraces, and narrow strips against a house wall. Whatever the situation, they must be massed so that the soil is completely hidden, but not so close that the plants cannot grow to their proper height and width. Always follow the cultural advice on the seed packets.

BELLIS (double daisy) Give them a cool, moist position if you want truly double flowers. 6 in, crimson, rose, salmon, white, giant or pompons.

CAMPANULA *pyramidalis*, (chimney bellflower) White and blue spires covered with starry bells, 3–4 ft. Good for borders and as pot plants.

DIGITALIS (foxglove) 'Foxy', 3–4 ft. Dwarfer and more compact and bushy than the ordinary type, with flowers in shades of carmine, pink, cream and white, with their lips attractively spotted. They remain in bloom a long time, particularly if the faded blooms are removed. (See page 37.)

FORGET-ME-NOT (*myosotis*) Indigo blue, dark and light blue, pink and white. 6–15 in. They generally re-sow themselves if you avoid hoeing or fussing around them, producing interesting colour variations the following year. If you want to replant and cultivate where the seeds would naturally germinate, pull up the plants before the seeds begin to drop and lay them in a shady place, out of the way where you are not likely to do any weeding, such as the base of a hedge. When the seedlings appear, transplant them wherever you wish. Alternatively, shake them where you want them to flower the following year, just as the seed pods are breaking open. They can be thinned out later.

HONESTY (*lunaria*) Purple and white, 2 ft. The flat silvery ornamental seed pods are in great demand for winter decoration. Their seedlings get scattered all around the garden, and can be easily transplanted or left to grow in their chosen new home. They must be cut for drying before their outer, disc coverings are discarded, as these protect them against rain. Once dry, you slip off the coverings between finger and thumb, saving the dark inner seed to sow later.

PENSTEMON Dwarf Hybrids: compact with short-stemmed clusters of pink, rose and lavender flowers, 9 in. *P. Heterophyllus*: spikes of brilliant blue flowers above slender grey-green foliate. To give its best it wants warm and light soil where it will grow into a fine 20-in plant.

SWEET WILLIAM Pink, crimson, harlequin and auricula-eyed. 6 in–$2\frac{1}{2}$ ft, sweetly scented. Clustered trusses on sturdy stems.

WALLFLOWER 6–18 in. Dwarf Tom Thumb varieties are particularly useful in exposed and windy positions. From strong single colours to pastel shades. They do actually enjoy a relationship with a wall. For best results, transplant seedlings to 6 in apart when they are 2–3 in high, and when they are growing strongly, pinch out the leading growths to make them bushy. Plant in final flowering positions during October and November, so they can establish a good root system before the soil cools down in winter.

Morning glory (*Ipomea tricolor* 'Praecox'). *See page 22.*

Hardy perennials

The following plants all need good well-drained soil, in a sunny position unless otherwise stated.

ACHILLEA (yarrow) Most varieties have flat yellow heads on stiff stems which makes them excellent flowers for cutting. The heads can be dried for winter use. Foliage is attractive, fern-like and pungent. Types vary in height from 1–4 ft. The flowers stay in good condition for months. They do not like the soil too rich.

ALCHEMILLA (lady's mantle) A great favourite with flower arrangers. Sprays of sulphur-yellow flowers and pretty leaves. 18 in. The flowers last a long time in water and can be dried as an everlasting. Cut the stems right back to the base leaves when they turn straw coloured and more will shoot up from the base. Once in your garden they are there to stay as they seed themselves – not so profusely as to be a nuisance.

ALSTROEMERIA (Peruvian lily) Lily-like trumpet flowers in a marvellous range of colours, they are among the aristocrats of border plants. Their claim to a place in this book is that they are 'easy' once they have taken to you, which may be a nerve-racking two years. Once they have made their decision, they will be with you for life if you leave them undisturbed. As the plants usually die down after transplanting, mark their positions with canes so that the white, tuberous roots are not accidentally dug into. Ligtu hybrids are delightful shades of pink, 2–3 ft tall. Good for cutting. Tricky to grow from seed.

ANCHUSA (borage) Brilliant masses of light and dark blue starry flowers which last a long time. Does not object to partial shade. Varieties range from 1–3 ft. Not a long liver so it is advisable to sow again from seed every 3 or 4 years.

ANEMONE (windflower) White, pink, rosy-red. The late-flowering *A. japonica* makes an excellent cut flower, $2\frac{1}{2}$ ft, quite unfussy and adaptable for both sun or semi-shade.

AQUILEGIA (columbine) Graceful, spurred flowers on slender

30

but stiff bushy stems which will not flop. Lovely clear colours in May and June. Will grow anywhere, $1\frac{1}{2}$–3 ft. (See page 40.)

ASTER (Michaelmas daisy) A great free-flowering family which provides a brilliant autumn display. Named varieties are a decided advance on the old wish-washy pale mauves and blues. For perfection they should be divided every year in spring, but this must depend on your particular priorities in life as well as the garden. There are bushy dwarfs and varieties up to 4 ft, some with flowers $2\frac{1}{2}$ in across in a marvellous range of colours The short, bushy types are extremely useful for the front of borders, edging paths and covering banks, as they need no supports, and keep their heads and dignity in the worst windy and wet weather.

CAMPANULA (bellflower) Huge family, purple, mauve, pink and white. Will grow in any soil, sun or shade, 1–4 ft. Specially recommended; *C. glomerata* 'Dahurica', bearing clustered heads of large rich violet bells on short stems; *C. lactiflora* 'Loddon Anna', with densely packed heads of lilac-pink; *C. persicifolia*, with graceful spikes of large blue bells which will last up to a fortnight when cut. (See page 81.)

CATANANCHE A real treasure. Long green stems bearing crisp silvery scaly buds. These open into exquisite cornflower-blue flowers with short yellow stamens. When the petals fade the flowerheads again resemble buds which can be dried for winter use. Give them a well-drained sunny place and they will flower from June to September. $2\frac{1}{2}$ ft. Best planted in spring.

CENTAUREA Pink, crimson and yellow, thistle-like flowers, 2–$3\frac{1}{2}$ ft. Attractive silvery foliage and excellent for cutting.

CHRYSANTHEMUM (maximum or Shasta daisy) Large white heads on strong 2–3 ft stems, some with either shaggy, frilled or double petals. Excellent for cutting, flowering over a long period from July to September. They like sunny, rich soil. C. Korean hybrids: single and semi-double flowers ranging in colour from pale pink to crimson and from primrose to deep

31

(*Above*) Love-lies-bleeding, amaranthus (*A. caudatus*) and (opposite) rock pinks, dianthus (*D. alpinus*) *See pages 23 and 34.*

bronze, with a host of in-between shades, $2\frac{1}{2}$–4 ft. August–November. Excellent for cutting and will stand a few degrees of frost. No disbudding and little staking.

DELPHINIUM Excellent results from seed. 'Belladonna': slender, branching type, ideal for flower arrangements, 2–3 ft, need no staking. White, pink and all shades of blue. 'Pacific Giants': an ever-blooming strain with massive spikes of large individual blooms $3\frac{1}{2}$ in across. 5 ft. Cut off the dead spikes and new ones will form.

DIANTHUS Much loved scented garden pinks. Particularly suitable for seaside areas. Sunny, well-drained position. 6 in–1 ft. Cut off the dead heads to keep the plants blooming.

DICTAMNUS *fraxinella* (burning bush or dittany) Bushy with spikes of rose or white flowers in early summer. The inflammable oil exuded from the glands of the flower stalks vaporizes and can be set alight on a still evening. Seed pods and leaves give off a wonderful scent if touched. 3 ft.

ERIGERON Very easy and pretty daisy flowers, pink, lilac and blue, with prominent yellow cushions of stamens. 2–$2\frac{1}{2}$ ft. The best varieties flower from June to October, and are not affected by bad weather.

ERYNGIUM (sea holly) Strikingly effective in the border or used fresh or dried in flower arrangements. Thistle-like flowers, mauve, pink, steel blue. 2–$2\frac{1}{2}$ ft.

EUPHORBIA (spurge) Unusual and full of character. Flower arrangers love their foliage. Several types from $1\frac{1}{2}$–3 ft. Specially recommended: *E. griffithii* 'Fire Glow', brilliant flame coloured heads May–August, $1\frac{1}{2}$ ft; *E. wulfernii*, a bold handsome plant with dense glaucous foliage and greeny-yellow flowers, 3 ft. It needs plenty of room to spread.

GERANIUMS (cranesbill) The true geraniums, not to be confused with the half-hardy summer bedding plants (pelargoniums).

They are wonderfully adaptable and will do well in any good soil, shade or sun. Make excellent ground cover. Small dainty flowers in blue, red, purple, pink, mauve, white shades, some with aromatic foliage. From 1–2½ ft. (See page 45.)

GEUM Exceptionally long flowering and popular flower, good for cutting. Shades of orange, red, apricot, yellow, 1–2 ft. They like ordinary, rather poor, soil. (See page 67.)

HELENIUM Easily grown, richly coloured, flowering throughout summer and autumn. Excellent for cutting. Bronze, crimson and yellow, 3–4 ft. They grow in most soils and situations, but do not like being over-baked.

HELLEBORUS Invaluable for decoration. Various types. The best known *H. niger* (the Christmas rose) is the least easy. Recommended: *H. corsicus*, unusual and striking plant for the winter border. Large bell-shaped creamy-green blooms hang on to the plant from mid-winter till April and longer. 2–3 ft. They like cool soil in dappled shade, and to be left severely alone; then seedlings will appear beneath them. These can be left, or transplanted when large enough to handle but will not flower till they are two years old. Never move a fully grown plant. Always hand weed. Never use a hoe or fork round their roots as they hate disturbance. *H. orientalis* (the Lenten rose): very like *H. corsicus* and needs the same treatment, but not so tall and imposing. Varied shades from pink to deep red on rigid stems from February to April. When the stamens have dropped the petals become 'petrified' and remain attractive for months while the seed pods develop. Seedlings produce many new and unexpected shades. *H. foetidus*: a choice, unusual plant producing an abundance of small green bell-shaped flowers on stout stems over a long period from early in the year. Handsome, hand-like dark foliage which is evergreen. Excellent for flower arrangements. The pale green seed pods are as striking as the flowers. Once introduced to a garden they will be there for ever for they produce carpets of seedlings, so you can try them out in a variety of situations. Not as fussy as the others, they will grow in full sun or shade, and come up among shrubs as happily as in a brick path. About 2 ft, but height varies with conditions. (See page 54.)

HEMEROCALLIS (day lily) Many new American hybrids, every shade except the blues and purples. They range from green, through apricot, pink, dark maroon to deep bronze. 2–3 ft. Flowers last only one day but are followed by many others over a long period. Very easy in sun or shade and any type of soil. They tolerate poor conditions, but look a great deal better when given plenty of humus and a feed. At the beginning of the planting season, and again after flowering, top-dress with well-rotted manure or a balanced fertilizer. Because of their dense foliage they make excellent ground cover if planted in groups, but are quite happy placed singly in a border. Be patient with them. It takes two or three years before they achieve maximum beauty and size of flower. Never disturb them or fork close to their roots. (See page 41.)

HOSTA (plantain lily, funkia) An increasingly popular foliage and ground cover plant. The flower spikes are generally lilac and unimportant rather than striking. None the less, both flowers and seed pods are much in demand by flower arrangers. Thrives in sun and shade; the variegated types prefer the shade. Rich well-manured soil is recommended but not essential. 2–2½ ft. (See page 139.)

IRIS Dwarf and tall bearded, in glorious colours. Easily grown in any sunny position where the ground has been well dug and cleared of perennial weeds, their worst enemies. Lime-lovers, they like a taste of mortar rubble, ground chalk or super-phosphate early in spring. Good drainage is essential. Rhizomes must only sit on the surface soil, so their backs can be baked in the sun, but firmly anchored below by their roots. They need splitting after a few years, replanting only the young, outer rhizomes.

KNIPHOFIA (red-hot-poker) Likes sun and dislikes cold wet soil. Many improved hybrids. Shades of yellow, orange and scarlet. The sword-like leaves can be tied round the crowns during

Foxglove (*Digitalis purpurea* 'Foxy'). *See page 27.*

winter, to prevent rain from rotting their centres. They are absolutely hardy. 2–4 ft. (See page 75.)

LUPIN Backbone of the border early in the season. Glorious colours. Bold groups are more effective than isolated specimens. Plant in full sun in soil which does not dry out. Remove dead heads to encourage a second flowering. Blooms last about five days in water if cut when the lowest flowers are just opening. $2\frac{1}{2}$–$3\frac{1}{2}$ ft. (See page 59.)

MONADA (bergamot) Aromatic leaves bearing turrets of flowers on leafy stems. Purple, crimson, pink and bright red. 2–3 ft. Plant in bold groups in full sun or light shade.

PAEONY White, pink, lilac, crimson, yellow, single and double. Fragrant. Plant in a deeply-dug and well-manured permanent position. They hate any disturbance around their roots. Plant with the tips of their crowns not more than 2 in below the soil surface. Deep planting stops them blooming. Gross feeders. Give a mulch of old manure in February and a dressing of bonemeal in autumn. 2–3 ft. (See page 55.)

PAPAVER (oriental poppy) No mixed border can make a show without them in May–June. A blaze of amazing colours. Art shades and named varieties with huge heads of salmon pink, scarlet, orange, pink, white, on strong furry stems. They like sun and any soil. Pick just before the buds are beginning to open for flower arrangements. The foliage gets untidy, but you can be ruthless and clear it right away when it browns. Give them later flowering neighbours to hide behind as they die away. 2–$3\frac{1}{2}$ ft.

PHLOX *paniculata* All colours except true blue and yellow. Long display of colour from July to October if planted where the soil does not dry out in summer. They particularly dislike the mid-day sun. $2\frac{1}{2}$–$3\frac{1}{2}$ ft.

POLEMONIUM (Jacob's ladder) Dainty bells of white, pink, blue and violet on stiff, upright spikes. Pretty foliage, 12–18 in.

Very useful as they flower for a long period and seed themselves.

PRIMULA An immense family which includes auriculas, cowslips, primroses and polyanthus. All need partial shade and moisture. 6–12 in.

PULMONARIA (lungwort, Jerusalem cowslip, soldiers and sailors) Most obliging plant, 6–9 in, March–April. Often has variegated or spotted leaves, bearing pink or blue flowers, sun or shade. The old-fashioned *P. officianalis* holds its white spotted leaves the year round, and become so tightly packed no weed can push through them. Very easy to divide and transplant.

RUDBECKIA (cone flower) One of the most free-flowering plants and invaluable for cutting. Orange, black and yellow eyed with a wonderful colour range in their wide petals. They like sun but will not resent a little shade.

SCABIOUS (pincushion flower) A most successful cut and border flower, but cannot survive in wet soil. It must be well-drained though not allowed to dry out in summer. 'Clive Greaves' is one of the finest for both border and house, soft blue, $2–2\frac{1}{2}$ ft. *S. Caucasica* 'Alba' is a pure white form, with frilly petals, $2–2\frac{1}{2}$ ft.

SEDUM Easily grown in any sunny place. Often called the 'ice plants' because of their unusual fleshy leaves. Butterflies are so attracted to the huge flat flower heads, that at certain times of the day the blooms are completely obscured by them. They flower just before the Michaelmas daisy season. Recommended for borders: *S. spectabile* 'Brilliant', deep bright pink with interesting and conspicuous grey fleshy leaves, 1 ft; 'Meteor', a glowing carmine-red, $1\frac{1}{2}$ ft; 'Autumn Joy', bright rose-salmon tinged bronze with massive heads, $1\frac{1}{2}–2$ ft. It may need some discreet propping up as the heavy stems are inclined to form a 'bowl' away from their centres. All are excellent for cutting.

SOLIDAGO (golden rod) This family has been much improved

(*Above*) Aquilegia (*A. hybrida*), and (*opposite*) day lily (Hemerocallis 'Pink Damask'). *See pages 30 and 36.*

by the hybridist during the last few years. The new varieties are still easy-going but not rampant and rather coarse as were the old ones. Yellow and gold, $2\frac{1}{2}$–$3\frac{1}{2}$ ft.

STACHYS *lanata* (lamb's ears) Dark rose flowers with silvery foliage. Its whitish woolly leaves form dense tufts which are attractive at all times. It produces spikes of small rose flowers during summer. 1–$1\frac{1}{2}$ ft. Quite indestructible, and does well in the poorest soils. Specially useful as ground cover.

THALICTRUM An extremely beautiful, dainty plant 4–5 ft. Tiers of tiny mauve bells with yellow stamens above delicate lacy foliage. Good for cutting. Does not like disturbance.

TRADESCANTIA (spiderwort, Moses-in-the-bulrushes) Too little grown. Ideal for sun or shade. The pretty three-cornered flowers bloom throughout summer, any soil. Shades of blue, violet-purple and bright red. $1\frac{1}{2}$–2 ft.

TROLLIUS (globe flower) Round, yellow, orange, lemon flowers on strong upright stems $1\frac{1}{2}$–$2\frac{1}{2}$ ft. Plant in moist soil, sun or shade. (See page 74.)

VERBASCUM (mullein) Elegant branching spires, often of most unusual shades and colouring. From June to August, 3–6 ft. Any soil in a sunny position. To ensure they have a long life, remove all their leaves as soon as they start to die in autumn. If left on they go soggy and rot the crown of the plant.

Alpine and rock plants

The plants in this section are for gardeners with Lilliputian tastes. They can be grown in orthodox rock gardens, sinks, paving or walls. Many of them can double up for other purposes, so if you have a surplus you can use them as edging or carpeting plants.

The important point is that where, and however, you want to grow these plants they must have good drainage and a

42

reasonably open, sunny place. In their native state most of them live on mountains, swept irregularly by torrents, and have to send their roots down for moisture as well as anchorage.

Many alpines prefer a slightly acid soil, with generous amounts of peat, leafmould, and the grit and soft sand which agrees with most of them. Quick acting fertilizers are not helpful, as they stimulate rapid and lush growth which is just what rock plants want least.

Some of the more adaptable rock plants look splendid massed in bold groups in the shrub or mixed border, or used as ground cover. The most reliable 'maids of all work' are found among the campanulas, helianthemums and hypericums.

ACHILLEA (yarrow) Gold, yellow and white flower clusters with narrow silvery leaves.

ALYSSUM (gold-dust) Trailers which produce sheets of yellow flowers, particularly suitable for draping rocks and walls. They contrast strikingly with arabis and aubrieta.

ARABIS (rock cress) Profusion of white or pink flowers.

ARMERIA (thrift) Particularly useful for paving and rock pockets, where there is plenty of sun. They form cushions of pink, red or white flowers.

ASTER *alpinus* Dwarf variety of Michaelmas daisy. Showy blue flowers with yellow centre, 6 in high and a spread of 12–18 in.

AUBRIETA A mass of colour during early spring for rambling over rocks or down the face of a dry wall. Sunny position. Many shades of pink, mauve, blue, lilac and crimson.

CAMPANULA (bellflower) Popular free-flowering family, 6–9 in, white, blue and mauve.

DIANTHUS (rock pinks) Plant in sunny, well-drained pockets. With a generous dressing of lime rubble, they give a long colourful and fragrant display. 6–9 in. (See page 33.)

DRYAS (mountain avens) A wide-spreading evergreen, with large, white, anenome-like flowers, followed by silken seed heads on slender stems. 3–5 in.

GENTIANA (gentian) *acaulis* Brilliant blue trumpets. 4 in. Tolerates lime but *must* be planted firmly.

GERANIUM (cranesbill) Dwarf varieties, 3–6 in. Do best in poor, gritty soil.

HELIANTHEMUM (rock rose) Shrubby trailing evergreen. Gives a brilliant show from June to September. Light soil. 6–10 in. Indispensable. Their only need is a hard cutting back after their main flowering is over, to encourage a second flowering in autumn.

IBERIS (perennial candytuft) Evergreen, white. Undemanding and indestructible.

PHLOX Alpine varieties. Brilliant cushions of bloom, 2–6 in.

POTENTILLA Beautiful golden-yellow flowers among tufts of glossy green leaves. 3 in.

ROSA (miniature rose) Tiny bushes, 4–12 in high.

SAXIFRAGE A large and important family. The Encrusted (or Silver) and Kabschia varieties need a sunny position. The Mossy varieties prefer a damp and shady situation.

SEDUM (stone-crop) Loves sun. Pink, purple, yellow flowers, 3–6 in. The succulent foliage makes it possible for them to withstand drought. (See page 127.)

SEMPERVIVUM (houseleek) Useful for massed, fleshy rosette effect. Some beautifully linked with cobweb tatting. Plant in crevices of rock for them to knit together.

SOLIDAGO *brachystachys* A miniature 9-in golden rod. Useful as a late flowerer with an undemanding nature.

Cranesbill geranium (*G. wallichianum* 'Buxton's Blue'). *See page 34.*

STACHYS *lanata* (lamb's ears) 'Silver Carpet'. A non-flowering form of silver-grey felted leaves. Good for ground cover and a foil for other plants. 4 in.

THYMUS (thyme) Yellow, silver, green fragrant foliage, with white, lavender, and red flowers. A substitute for summer flowering heathers if your soil is limy. The *Serpyllum*, prostrate, forms are good in or around paving.

VERONICA (speedwell) Dwarf-growing, trailing plants, blue, pink and mauve, 4–6 in.

3 BULBS ROUND THE YEAR

There is no month of the year when it is not possible to have some kind of hardy bulb flowering outside in the garden. Once planted, they will be with you for life. The most important decision to make is where to put what, so you can see them when they flower, and where to place them so they can be left permanently to multiply.

The following list will not include any bulbs which need to be lifted and stored in winter, or those which are used as bedding plants. They may be easy if you are employed full-time by the parks department of the local council, but when gardening is a small corner of an over-crowded life, they do not qualify for inclusion.

First, to get rid of the differences between what is a bulb, corm or tuber. Bulbs, such as hyacinths and lilies, have fleshy scales packed on top of each other, as you see when cutting an onion in half. These scales are really storage houses. They wrap round and feed the embryo flower within.

A corm is solid right through and is a thickened stem, with the embryo flower bud on the surface at the corm's apex. Crocus and gladioli are examples.

Tubers are also solid flesh, such as cyclamen; aconites and colchicum are swollen roots; while rhizomes are swollen stems growing horizontally, e.g., iris.

The important common factor is that they store their food as if their lives depend on it, which it does, literally. So they can hibernate without injury for long winter months when growing conditions are unfriendly. Though you cannot starve

them, you can drown them. Never plant them where the ground might become waterlogged in winter.

There are few places in the garden which cannot be improved with bulbs imaginatively planted. Under hedges, among shrubs, round trees. The variation in habit, shape, size, colour, different seasons of blooming, makes them one of the easiest of all ornamental plants. Some are expensive – because they are difficult to propagate – so if you keep to the cheaper varieties, you can be sure they will last in the garden indefinitely, increasing all the time.

Spring bulbs undoubtedly look their best planted informally in grass or rock gardens. But they must be strictly informal, grouped in drifts or patches. Avoid at all costs soldier-stiff rows of daffodils along a path, or large Dutch crocus making tram lines round the edge of a small rectangular lawn.

Before you plant bulbs anywhere you want them to remain, multiply and be completely 'no-trouble' plants, think about their leaves. The small early spring bulbs will have died out of sight by the time you want to cut the grass, but daffodils are another matter. They are best naturalized in rough grass which can be left uncut till the leaves start to turn brown. As with all bulbs, corms, etc., the leaves must die down to restock the larder for winter.

Another way of disguising the messy death of permanently planted bulbs is to put them among shrubs whose foliage will hide them. Or if the lawn is large enough, have contrasting heights of grass, so that circles around trees or irregular patches and drifts, can be left long and bulb-planted to skirt and form a pattern among the closely mown grass. Like embossed velvet.

It is a waste of time to knot daffodil leaves in the hope they will die down more quickly; you merely waste it and create a hideously unnatural sight.

Cultivation
Good drainage is the most important factor in planting bulbs. If naturalized, they can be dibbed in the ground, or a layer of turf lifted. the undersoil lightly forked, the bulbs spaced irregularly and the turf replaced. This is the best method with

Dog's tooth violet (*Erythronium dens-canis* 'Rose Queen'). *See page 50.*

large bulbs. The depth of planting depends on the size of the bulbs. As a general guide they should have the same depth of soil over their noses as the depth of the bulb measures from shoulder to base. If the soil is poor, add a scatter of general fertilizer, at the rate given by the manufacturer, before planting. Or you can use compost or manure if it is absolutely decomposed; otherwise it will scorch the bulbs.

Caution
A novice bulb buyer should send for a specialist bulb catalogue. Over-the-counter bulbs in general shops (not garden centres) have often been exposed to variable heat and light and will be past their best. Beware, too, of bargain offers late in the season for that particular variety.

Spring bulbs

CHIONODOXA (glory of the snow) Dainty, brilliant blue and mauve, starry-eyed little flowers, 5 in. They should be planted generously for a good impact. There is also a white and a pink variety.

CROCUS A large number of species, delicate in texture, free-flowering, with an astonishing range of colour and combinations, from brown-yellow to yellow-violet. These are much less coarse than the flamboyant Dutch forms, so need to be planted where you can see or pass them closely. They are not for long-distance viewing.

CYCLAMEN *coum* Crimson, pink and white, some with marbled leaves, 3 in, perfectly hardy, from December till March. Plant in light shade, preferably under deciduous trees or shrubs where they will not be disturbed and can multiply.

ERANTHIS (winter aconite) Makes a golden lake of colour under shrubs and in grass, where the leaves which follow later can die down without giving offence. Good in a paeony bed where they can multiply, as neither likes disturbance. 3–4 in.

ERYTHRONIUM (dog's tooth violet) A graceful group. The dog's

Anemone (*A. coronaria* 'De Caen'). *See page 53.*

tooth violet has cyclamen-like flowers and two broad leaves which are a lovely green mottled with reddish-brown. Flowers variable from white to pink and violet, 5 in. Does well in sun or shade, but objects to being baked. (See page 48.)

FRITILLARIA (snake's head) Meleagris varieties produce mysterious effects naturalized in shady grass or under trees. The distinctive hanging bells are on graceful 12-in stems, in shades from creamy white to purple with greenish tones. (See page 79.)

GALANTHUS (snowdrop) White and green, single and double, 6 in. Plant with bulbs touching in semi-shade. They are best planted or re-planted immediately they have flowered, before the leaves die down. *G. Elwesii*, 7 in, a distinct species with large snowy-white globular flowers, and stronger larger blue-grey leaves than the common types. They flower better in full sun.

HYACINTH Wonderful shades and heavy scent. 1 ft. Particularly useful among shrubs.

TULIP A large family with surprising diversity of colour and shape. Recommended Botanical Tulips (species). The dwarf and very early *kaufmannianas*, 8 in, with their delightful colouring, and the *greigiis* with beautiful mottled leaves and brilliant flowers should be in every garden. They open their faces flat to the sun. They naturalize freely without needing any special attention, and are ideal in rockeries or borders where they can remain undisturbed. Early singles and doubles on their short sturdy stems are excellent under shrubs where they can be left alone.

Summer bulbs

ALLIUM The onion family includes the most splendid decorative kinds. The seedpods are as striking as their flowers, and most distinctive when dried for winter use. Very versatile, they can be used as eye-catchers in almost any part of the garden – in borders, rockeries, grass, under trees, in a great variety of colours, habits, heights and flowering times. Plant at a depth equal to twice the diameter of the bulb. All shapes, colours and sizes from 6 in–3 ft, blue, yellow, rose, white, carmine, solid or tasselled. Beware of putting the 10 in *A. moly* into a mixed border. It is a traveller, and spreads rapidly. It flowers in June, and the compact umbels of bright yellow flowers are best naturalized where no digging is necessary.

ANEMONE *coronaria* '*St Brigid*' and '*de Caen*' Rich colours. 7–10 in, single and double. (See page 51.)

CAMASSIA 2–3 ft flower stems packed with pale blue star-like blossoms between May and July. Plant the large bulbs $\frac{3}{4}$ in deep and about 6 in apart in September and October. They can stand wetter conditions than most bulbs and make handsome border plants or can be naturalized in grass. Established clumps should be left undisturbed. Very good as cut flowers – the buds open in water.

CYCLAMEN *neapolitanum* Late summer, white and pink, 3–5 in.

FRITILLARIA *imperialis* (crown imperial) One of the most important, unusual and beautiful plants, the big brother of the snakeshead fritillaria, which likes to be naturalized. Crown imperial is a majestic border plant, with large yellow and orange, pendulous bell flowers, surmounted by a green crown of leaves. They grow 2–3 ft, and flower in May. Leave all the foliage till it dies back, then pull it off and mark the spot so you don't accidentally stab the bulbs when they are out of sight, then they will multiply.

GALTONIA (summer hyacinth, spire lily) White, 3–4 ft spikes tightly packed with large, fragrant, hanging pure white flowers each about $1\frac{1}{2}$ in long. They bloom between August– September, and need deep, rich well-drained soil in full sun. Once established they should be left alone.

LILIUM *candidum* (Madonna lily) The oldest lily cultivated in Europe. It produces pure satin-white chalice-like flowers of exceptional fragrance on stems 3–4 ft in June–July. Thoroughly easy-going, even in lime, good grouped in mixed borders and excellent as cut flower. *L. regale*, for 'starter' gardeners.

53

(*Above*) Corsican hellebore (*H. corsicus*) and (*opposite*) paeony (*P. Mlokosewitschii*). *See pages 35 and 38.*

Most accommodating of all lilies, in light and heavy soils, with or without lime. In July the strong, flexible 3–4 ft stems are crowned with large funnel-shaped flowers, pure white inside, the back of the petals streaked brown. Pervading scent in July. Thrives in sun or partial shade, and can be naturalized. Invaluable as a cut flower.

MONTBRETIA 1–3 ft, bearing streams of tubular flowers, yellow, orange, copper, red. July–September. Very useful as clumps in borders, at the base of light hedges and among shrubs. Dainty and long lasting as cut flowers.

Autumn and winter bulbs

COLCHICUM (meadow saffron) Most showy of autumn flowers. They get their nickname 'naked ladies', by suddenly appearing from the ground without any under- or over-wear. A most striking sight, huge, 6-in crocus-like blooms, mostly rose-carmine, single, double and waterlily flowered. Easy to grow, but not so easy to place because of the large spinach-like foliage, 18 in, which follows the demise of the ladies in spring. It must be left to send nourishment back to the bulbs, and is a very messy sight when it turns yellow. They do well and multiply in full sun or partial shade, can be naturalized easily and are suited to wild gardens, the fringe of woodlands or around and under shrubs. They flower shortly after being planted in late July or August.

CROCUS *speciosus* Bursts into flower in early September, in a wide range of colours. They resemble their dainty spring-flowering counterparts, and are particularly good for naturalizing. Mixtures offered for sale are good, but for continuous flowering choose named species.

NERINE *bowdenii* Spectacular deep pink umbels of flowers on $2\frac{1}{2}$-ft stems, with long, strap-shaped leaves. They like a well-drained spot, preferably against a south wall, where they can be left alone to colonize. Split them only if they are obviously deteriorating from being overcrowded. Plant with their noses only just below soil-level.

56

4 FLOWERING SHRUBS

Shrubs have become the 'maids of all work' in both small and grand gardens, for the obvious reason that *they* work for you rather than *you* for them. They are permanent inhabitants, entirely under your control.

They can be used individually, as focal points, planted on their own with undercoverings of permanent bulbs or carpeting plants, or in a mixed border where they will be the stabilizers among the different groups.

Because shrubs are so easy to grow, it does not follow that you can just drop them in a hole in the ground and let them get on with it. Nothing is going to stay with you permanently unless you make it welcome.

When possible, the area or single spot, where shrubs are to be planted should be dug and prepared a few months before planting, so that the soil can settle.

Preparing and planting
Dig the ground deeply, removing any perennial weeds, and break up the sub-soil. Once established, most shrubs have few needs and flourish in a wide variety of soil conditions. Rhododendrons, azaleas, camellias and other lime-haters like a little leafmould, peat, well-decayed manure or garden compost worked into the bottom spit. Soils which are light and porous are improved by adding strawy manure, old compost and any fibrous material which will help to retain moisture. Deciduous shrubs can be moved from late October to early April; evergreens transplant most successfully in September, October and from March to early May.

The planting holes should be wider than the spread of the roots, and the soil pressed in firmly to anchor them, so that wind will not rock and tear the fine feeding roots away from their 'larder'. It is really a two-man-woman job – one to hold the shrub in position and wiggle it as the other puts back the soil and firms it so there are no soil pockets. To make sure of getting the right depth of planting, put a stick across the top of the hole. The soil mark on the stem made at the nursery should be slightly above this to allow for the shrinkage and settling of the new soil. Grafted shrubs must not be planted too deeply, or they will send up endless troublesome suckers.

Most shrubs will benefit by being planted in a mixture of equal parts of sifted soil, peat or leafmould, or bonfire ash. Keep this mixture in a dry place (heavy duty plastic sack), so that if your soil is damp and sticky when the plants arrive, you can still go ahead with planting.

Though the majority of shrubs are unfussy, it is a waste of time attempting to grow rhododendrons, azaleas, camellias and certain ericas if your soil is limy. They need an acid, peaty soil. You can help them along with doses of Sequestrene, but they will only exist, reluctantly, in treated alkaline soil.

Many evergreen shrubs, including rhododendrons, arrive from the nursery, or are bought from garden centres, with their roots in a sacking 'snood'. Leave this on when you put them in their planting holes, as it will soon rot away and the roots grow through. But don't forget to cut the ties that secure it round the stem.

It sometimes happens that a shrub stays dormant after planting for such a long time that you wonder if it is alive. You can find out by lightly scratching the bark with a finger nail. If it is green, it is still alive. Start with the top branches, and if these are dead, work your way down until you, hopefully, come to living growth, then cut off the dead parts.

Don't fall into the trap of planting shrubs too closely in a hurry for a quick show of colour. Find out their eventual height and width before you put them in. Although you are the boss and keep them tamed by pruning, their natural character and shape will be altered; as well as giving you much unnecessary work.

58

Russell Lupin: hybrid lupins such as these are not strictly 'easy' since they are comparatively short lived, but they are well worthwhile as they are available in a glorious range of colour. *See page 38.*

In a border or bed of shrubs, the spaces left for the larger-growing ones to develop to full size, can be filled with shorter, expendable, quick-growing, short-lived stop-gaps such as lavender, hypericum, artemesia, and brooms, which can be removed without too much heartache, when the time comes.

As a general guide, low-growing and medium-sized shrubs are spaced up to 5 ft apart, and more vigorous ones 10–15 ft. This looks a bit mean in the early days, and whether you follow the advice or not will depend on your planning a long- or short-term garden.

Shrubs

BERBERIS *thunbergii* Reddish-yellow flowers, April–May, followed by large red berries. Splendid autumn colour. 4–6 ft. Thin out overcrowded shoots after flowering or during winter. Leave any drastic pruning till February.

BUDDLEIA (butterfly bush) New varieties are richly coloured, white, mauve, purple. 6–8 ft. Does well in towns in sunny position. July–August. Cut back previous season's growth to within a few inches of the old wood every February–March. *B. globosa*, the 'orange ball tree' needs plenty of room, 8–15 ft. Bears fragrant orange flowers the size and shape of large marbles. Semi-evergreen, thrives at seaside, June. May be cut back in May if necessary.

CARYOPTERIS (blue spiraea) 4–5 ft, August–September. Cut back previous summer's shoots hard annually at the end of March.

CHIMONANTHUS (winter sweet) One of the finest winter-flowering scented shrubs, bearing pale yellow bell-shaped flowers in January. 5 ft. Cut sprays will fill a room with fragrance. Warm, sheltered site. No regular pruning. (See page 62.)

CHOISYA (Mexican orange blossom) Pure white, sweetly scented, May–June, 4–6 ft. Glossy evergreen foliage. Tolerates shade.

COTONEASTER Many distinct types, mostly evergreens, remarkable for their berries.

CYDONIA (chaenomeles; japonica) The flowering Japanese quince thrives in any well-drained soil and any aspect, against walls or an open border. Rose, pink, orange, crimson. They often flower from February to May and again in autumn. All varieties bear crops of yellow or green ornamental fruit which can be used for jelly or wine making. Prune back long summer shoots in September–October.

CYTISUS (broom) White and yellow sun lovers, sometimes short-lived. Lightly prune immediately after flowering to prevent shrub from becoming straggly. Specially recommended: *C. battandieri*, an unusual and striking shrub for growing against a wall, 5–12 ft. Handsome, silvery semi-evergreen leaves, and tight sprays of golden-yellow pineapple scented flowers in June–July. Needs a wind-sheltered place in the sun. A south wall is perfect. Train and prune after flowering. (See page 63.)

DAPHNE *mezereum* Renowned for fragrance of flowers which appear before the leaves. Likes cool, preferably alkaline soil in shade. 3–4 ft. Against a north wall it can flower from Christmas till April. No pruning.

DEUTZIA White and purple, 4–8 ft, June. Good shrubs for town. Cut back old flowered wood to healthy new growth after flowering. Leave young shoots unpruned.

DIERVILLA (weigela) Showy trumpet flowers, pink and red. 5 ft, May and June. Cut back the flowered wood to healthy new growth as soon as the blooms fade.

FORSYTHIA A choice of yellow and golden varieties, 6–10 ft, March–April. Shorten all shoots which have flowered.

FUCHSIA Hardy varieties, red, 3–10 ft, particularly suitable for seaside gardens. They often need pruning almost to ground level in spring, when strong new shoots will break from the

(*Above*) Winter sweet (*Chimonanthus praecox* 'Luteus') and (*opposite*)
Moroccan broom (*Cytisus battandieri*). *See pages 60 and 61.*

crowns of the bushes. Flowering continuously from early summer to late autumn.

HYDRANGEA Blue, white, pink, red. *H. paniculata grandiflora* has white flowers, August–September, flushed with pink as they age. 6–8 ft. Rich, moist soil. Prune in March, removing all weak shoots and reducing last year's shoots by half.

HYPERICUM Tremendously useful family, which includes the 'rose of Sharon', for sun or shade, flowering for a long time. Particularly good as ground cover, among shrubs or on banks. Gold and yellow flowers, 3–5 ft, July–August. (See page 85.)

KERRIA *japonica* (Jew's mallow) An old-fashioned favourite for any soil or situation. A profusion of double or single yellow flowers, April–May. 4–6 ft. Makes a shapely bush. Remove oldish wood after flowering.

LAVENDULA (lavender) Evergreys. Particularly good for formal planting on patios, against walls, as edgings and hedgings. 3 ft, many shades of blue and purple. Clip over annually in August when the flowers are spent. Leave about an inch of the new growth made during the summer.

MAHONIA *japonica* Shiny evergreen foliage, beautiful at all times of the year. 3–5 ft, sheltered from cold winds. Fragrant sulphur-yellow, lily-of-the-valley like sprays in winter. Use peat when planting. Takes time to settle in.

PAEONIA (tree paeony) These shrubby paeonies are among the most showy garden plants in April–June. Many varieties, small single flowers, to huge double ones of soup plate size, 3–7 ft tall in every shade but blue. They like a rich, well-dug soil, and no digging or disturbance round their roots once established. They need no pruning, but dead wood should be cut away in spring. Wonderful cut flowers. Unlike the herbaceous members of the family, tree paeonies must be planted 3–4 in deep.

PHILADELPHUS (mock orange) Often wrongly called 'syringa',

64

which is actually the generic name of the 'lilac'. Easily grown in sun or shade. Masses of white scented blossom in June–July. Many forms, 3–15 ft, with small or large, single and double flower sprays. Thin out shoots which have flowered as soon as the blooms die.

POTENTILLA (shrubby cinquefoil) Yellow, 2–4 ft, June–September. They do best in a sunny, open position, but can put up with a little shade and any kind and quality of soil. No pruning needed. Old wood and overcrowded shoots can be cut out in September–October.

RHUS (stag's horn sumach) 12–15 ft. Very good for poor soil but has a nasty habit of sending up suckers yards away, so not a good specimen for lawn. Needs no attention except to remove any dead wood or branches that spoil the shape.

RIBES (flowering currant) White, pink, crimson and a yellow variety, *R. aureum*. 6 ft, April. Completely unfussy.

ROMNEYA (Californian tree poppy) Large, sweetly scented butterfly-wing white petals surrounding conspicuous golden stamens. July–October. 4–5 ft. The vigorous shoots are clothed with blue-green poppy-like foliage which dies down in winter. It thrives best in full sun with its roots close to a wall.

ROSA Shrub roses come in all sizes, from about 2 to 15 ft. They can be used as handsome specimens on their own, in mixed plantings with others of their kind or with other shrubs, and some will mix quite happily with non-shrubby border plants. They can be spreading and sprawling, bushy, or erect and upright. A few give rich autumn colouring with their leaves, others have fragrant foliage. All have beautiful, and some really sumptuous flowers, in most cases scented, which are often followed by decorative hips in autumn in a vast variety of shapes and colours. The great advantage of them is that unlike the hybrid teas and floribundas, they have very long lives and need almost no attention. No dead-heading (you would lose the autumn berries), no regular pruning, just cut out the dead wood when necessary.

Shrub roses include all the old-fashioned types, sweet briars, *spinosissima*, rugosa, musk, moss, China, Bourbon, damask, *gallica*, as well as the modern shrub roses, of which they are the parents. Some well-proved varieties include:

Canary Bird Bright yellow, single, May–June, 6 ft.

Fargesii Bright pink flowers in summer followed in August by long red hips.

Frühlingsgold Light yellow semi-double flowers in May, 6–8 ft.

Hybrid Sweet Penzance briars Very vigorous, fragrant foliage.

Moss roses Fragrant, 4–6 ft, white, pink, creamy crimson.

Damask rose, York and Lancaster The true historical variety, usually striped pale pink and white. Rather large and straggling.

Nevada The almost thornless branches sparkle with hundreds of pale pink buds opening to semi-double creamy white flowers 5 in across. A dazzling sight in May–June, again in August and intermittently onwards. 7 ft.

Perle d'Or A China rose. Rich yolk yellow buds, apricot flowers fading to cream. 3 ft.

Pink Grootendorst A long-flowering rugosa sport, the flowers resembling a clear pink picotee-edged dianthus. Good for cutting. 4 ft.

Souvenir de la Malmaison, Bourbon Pale blush pink flowers fading almost white; powerful fragrance. Large cupped flowers, maturing flat and quartered, up to 5 in across. 6 by 5 ft.

Modern shrub roses

1 *Summer flowering*
'Celestial' (Céleste) Clear pink
'Complicata' Bright pink, white centre
'Constance Spry' Bright rose pink, scented
'Fritz Nobis' Salmon pink
'Frühlingsmorgen' Rose pink, yellow centre
'Golden Chersonese' Deep pink
'Maiden's Blush' Pale pink
R. pteragonis 'Cantabrigiensis' Pale yellow.

Geum (*G.* × *borisii*). *See page 35.*

2 *For hips as well as flowers*
R. *caudata* Red flowers, orange-red hips
R. *davidii* Pink flowers, scarlet hips.
R. 'Geranium' Scarlet flowers, crimson hips
R. *highdownensis* Crimson flowers, orange-red hips
R. *holodonta* Light pink flowers, scarlet hips
R. *moyessi* Usually blood-red flowers, orange-red hips (See page 89)
R. *multibracteata* Pink flowers, small orange-red hips
R. *rubifolia* Pink flowers, red hips, blue-grey foliage
R. *scabrosa* Mauve-pink flowers, large bright red hips
R. *sweginzowii* Pink flowers, orange-red hips, early.

3 *Repeat flowering*
'Blanc Double de Coubert' White, fragrant (See page 88)
'Buff Beauty' Apricot yellow
'Chinatown' Pink with yellow base
'Cornelia' Pink with yellow base
'Fred Loads' Vermilion-orange
'Heidelberg' Bright red
'Joseph's Coat' Yellow, orange and red
'Marguerite Hilling' Deep pink
'Nymphenburg' Salmon pink
'Penelope' Creamy salmon.

SENECIO Indestructible silver-grey, all year round foliage, 3 ft, with white or yellow daisy-like flowers in July. The felt-like sprays of leaves much used by flower arrangers.

SPIRAEA Large family, varied in height, habit and colour. Mostly white, pink and crimson, 3–8 ft. They flower on new growth, so cut back some of the shoots after flowering.

SYRINGA (lilac) White, mauve, purple, primrose, wonderfully scented. They flower better if you can find time to cut off dead flower heads and remove any suckers at the base.

VIBURNUM *fragrans* Wonderfully scented flowers, pale pink in bud opening to white, November–February, 7–8 ft.

5 CLIMBERS AND WALL PLANTS

Knowing just how climbers climb is essential before deciding what and where to plant them. Only a few do so naturally. They have to be encouraged up, round, or through some permanent host or structure. Some have to be tied to their supports, others will send out tendrils to do it themselves, often, clutching at 'straws in the wind', they will entwine themselves into a neighbouring plant which is far from pleased by such familiar goings on. Clematis are particular culprits. They must have their own climbing frame, otherwise they will take to anything they can lay hands on, at a high and low level.

Climbing plants can be used to clothe what is bare or disguise what is ugly. These may be walls, fences, storage tanks, or a dead tree stump. In choosing what to put where, don't waste a precious sunny wall on something which would grow equally well against a shaded one. Reserve the favoured places for the fusspots who need them. Consider which way the climber will face and what protection it will have. Some climbers need sun, others don't. Some can stand cold winds, others can't. Some like their feet hot, others cold.

There is a wide choice of supports for climbers. The wooden trellis has largely given way to lightweight plastic-covered metal which is fitted to walls with ingenious clips; or there are vine guides, plastic netting, or simply wire stretched between nails.

The soil at the foot of a wall is usually poor, owing to the accumulation of builders' rubble and sub-soil. It is also usually dry because of overhanging eaves. Before planting, dig out the existing soil and replace it with better soil from some other part of the garden, mixing in plenty of organic manure of the kind you can buy in bags at your local garden shop.

Any heights given can be only approximate, as this will depend very much on the soil, position and treatment your climbers are given.

Climbing plants

AKEBIA *quinata* Semi-evergreen twiner with very attractive five-fingered foliage, 8–15 ft. Chocolate-purple, scented flowers in April, followed in autumn by intriguing sausage-like fruits, grey-violet. Any fertile soil. South-west aspect.

CELASTRUS *orbiculatus* Vigorous twiner useful for covering tree stumps or unsightly objects. Yellow leaves in autumn and decorative scarlet seeds in yellow cases which last throughout the winter. Any position.

CLEMATIS *montana* White and rose-pink small flowers with prominent yellow stamens. Very vigorous, free-flowering twiner in May. Any position. *C. tangutica*: a delightful twiner and the best yellow-flowered clematis. Slender but strong growths in autumn produce an abundance of small lantern-shaped, rich yellow flowers, the later ones intermingling with masses of feathery seed heads. Any aspect. Only prune, if too rampant, after flowering. (See opposite.)

The large-flowered hybrids are less easy to establish than the above species, and are decidedly fussy, so have regretfully been excluded from this book.

HEDERA (ivy) There is no other self-clinging evergreen to match it. Thrives in almost any soil or situation in an infinite variety of forms. Stays beautiful through all seasons. Look for the silver and variegated forms rather than the gloomy green-leaved species. Besides their superior appearance, their leaves contain less chlorophyll and so are less rampant. Contrary to the rumours spread by non-ivy lovers, it does not harm sound structures or healthy trees. Ivy takes the blame for a

70   Clematis (*C. tangutica*). Easier to grow than the large flowered hybrids.
See above.

crumbling wall and a dying tree because its healthy foliage disguises the fact. Plant in spring and pinch back young shoots in June to encourage branching. Clip those on walls in April to keep neat.

HYDRANGEA *petiolaris* (climbing hydrangea) A north wall need never be dull, for the climbing hydrangea prefers them to hotter spots. The flat heads of white flowers, 6 in or more across, smother the plants June–July. Self-clinging, any aspect but south. Slow starter until established, then speeds up. 10 ft by 12 ft.

JASMINUM *officinale* (common jasmine) One of the oldest and most easily cultivated plants. A strong-growing, semi-evergreen twiner, producing white fragrant flowers from June to September. Rapid grower. Does best on a south or west wall, but will also grow on a north one. 8 ft, but will reach 30 ft if trained. *J. officinale* 'Grandiflorum' has pink shaded buds opening white in summer.

LONICERA (honeysuckle) All climbing members of the family are worth cultivating, though not all have the fragrance and beauty of our common hedgerow species. They are probably seen at their best rambling over other bushes or tree stumps, but are very adaptable. Many like half-shade or even complete shade and are then less susceptible to aphis. There are many kinds, pink, yellow, cream, coral, red, both deciduous and evergreen, flowering from June to September. They prefer a good loamy soil and plenty of moisture. Seldom at their best against a wall, and where possible, should ramble over a pergola or arch, or cover unwanted trees or unsightly sheds. All are twiners. Trim with shears and thin old wood when necessary.

PARTHENOCISSUS *henryana* Beautiful self-clinging foliage plant, related to the Virginia creeper, and famous for the beauty of the vine-like leaves which turn to dazzling red and crimson hues in autumn. Best in shade, when the leaves have an attractive network of white and purple variegation.

72

PASSIFLORA *caerulea* (passion flower) This is so beautiful and remarkable, it is worthy of your best warm wall. Grows to 20 ft in poor, well-drained soil and sheltered spot. A vigorous quick-grower, it climbs by means of tendrils. The fragrant intriguing purple flowers, 3–4 in wide, start to appear in June and continue till September, followed by orange 'egg' fruits.

POLYGONUM *baldschuanicum* (Russian vine) The 'mile-a-minute' Russian vine will smother an outhouse, or anything unsightly, or clothe a large tree in the shortest possible time, growing 15 ft a season. Sensational from July to October, when it is covered in a froth of panicles, cream faintly tinted pink. Good on wire netting.

SOLANUM *jasminoides* Twining member of the potato family. Slender, fast-growing, semi-evergreen. The clusters of palest slate-blue flowers with orange eyes start to appear about mid-summer and continue until checked by frost. 12 ft, any soil, but must have a sheltered wall in full sun and a south or west aspect.

VITIS (vine family) Easy in any soil or position, noted for their beautiful autumn colouring and the wealth of variation in form and foliage. They attach themselves by twining tendrils. *V. coignetiae*, the grandest of all ornamental vines: leaves often 12 in across with a buff reverse make a gorgeous autumn display of brilliant shades (see page 105.) The flower clusters, although small, are extremely sweet-smelling, June–July, followed by small purple grapes. No pruning needed unless space is limited. *V. unifera* 'Brandt'. The leaves of this edible hardy variety turn crimson, pink and orange in autumn; the grapes are purple black. *V. unifera* 'Purpurea', the 'teinturier grape'. The leaves are at first a claret red, turning deep vinous purple later. Most effective in contrast with grey or silver foliage. These two varieties will reach 10–15 ft and should be pruned in early winter. Once the allotted area has been covered, prune laterals hard back to two or three eyes from their base; weak, straggling shoots to one bud. Sturdy shoots needed for exten-sion, reduce by one-third.

(*Above*) Globeflower, trollius (*T. europaeus*) and (*opposite*) red-hot-poker
(*Kniphofia galpinii*). *See pages 42 and 36.*

WISTERIA *sinensis* Moisture loving, vigorous twiner, producing laburnum-like, fragrant, lilac-blue flowers before the leaves in spring. They prefer lime-free soil and sunny walls. When established prune projecting trails back to 2 in in August. Excellent for archways and pergolas. The flowers display themselves best when hanging away from walls, on short shoots which develop with pruning. Left unpruned, wisterias develop into a thick tangle of intertwining stems which do not flower. They remain dormant for months following transplanting and the buds may not break until late June or early July. The buds can be encouraged to break by spraying overhead with lukewarm water on warm, still days.

Rambling and climbing roses

There is an infinity of choice, the most difficult decision being to get the right rose for the purpose you want. Covering house walls is, on the whole, the least satisfactory way of using them. Vigorous winds can turn their long thorny branches into destructive lashes, which damage plaster and woodwork, as well as people.

Repeat flowering climbers, most of which are of quite recent origin can be used in the same ways as other climbing plants. They have almost ousted the large-flowered hybrid tea climbers which have a comparatively short flowering period, and a nasty habit of going bare below the knees.

Apart from their use as quick-growing screens, for pergolas, pillars and trellises, climbing and rambling roses make ideal lodgers. They use other plants already in your garden as their clothes horses.

Flowering shrubs are perfect for this if you choose the association carefully; getting heights, colours and flowering times in harmony, so that you do not have to cut back one at an inconvenient time for the other.

Many new gardens contain mature trees which have mercifully been left by the developers. Others include trees which have lost their charm, such as old plums which have ceased to

76

fruit but make mysterious winter silhouettes. Even if you wanted them down, the high cost of felling would be enough to encourage you to learn to live with them.

Ornamental trees can become repeat-flowering with roses scrambling through them. A flowering cherry, for instance, is little more than a mass of dark foliage once its springtime explosion is past. But it can sparkle brilliantly for the rest of the year, often well into winter, with a vigorous climber such as 'Mermaid' threading among the leafy branches with its large, single, canary-yellow blooms. Viburnums and philadelphus (mock orange) make excellent, though more modest, frame-work.

As a general guide, the more rampant the growth, the shorter the flowering period tends to be, as is the case with ramblers. They have one grand flowering spree, often lasting for a month, and immediately afterwards devote their energies to producing new canes from the base on which the following season's one crop of flowers will be borne.

Pruning

Ramblers Cut out old flowered growth from the base any time after flowering, and tie in the new shoots. If you want a larger plant, the younger growth should be used to furnish the lower parts, and some of the older wood left to drape over or climb through the heights.

Climbers In March, or after flowering in summer, remove enough growths over two years old to prevent them from being too crowded. Prevent the base becoming bare by shortening back one or two of the older shoots every four years.

Ramblers, once-flowering

Albertine June–July. Deep coppery red buds opening to fragrant salmon-pink full flowers which smother the vigorous flowers of last year. Needs no pruning unless it gets out of hand.

Chaplin's Pink Companion Bright pink, semi-double flowers with golden stamens. Glossy, leathery dark green foliage.

Crimson Shower Small semi-double crimson flowers, flowering late over a long period.

Emily Gray Pointed buds, rich golden buff, deeper in the heart; opening flat, semi-double, in small trusses. Very fragrant.

Paul's Scarlet Climber Bright scarlet-red, profuse bloom, semi-double clusters.

All-purpose climbers and ramblers
Altissimo Velvety red, repeat flowering with single flat-faced flowers revealing brilliant golden stamens.

Bantry Bay Repeat flowering, light rose-pink blooms in masses throughout summer, with dense medium-green foliage. Vigorous, 10–12 ft.

Danse du Feu Repeat flowering. 10 ft. Bright orange-red semi-double blooms. Will grow on a north wall.

Dortmund Repeat flowering. 10–12 ft. Large single blooms of red with white centres borne in large clusters.

Golden Showers Repeat flowering. Dainty buds opening to large flat bright yellow blooms. Will grow on a north wall.

Handel Repeat flowering. Dainty creamy-white edged with rose-pink. 10 ft.

Joseph's Coat Repeat flowering. A restrained grower, yellow, orange and red with pale green foliage.

Marigold Semi-double, very fragrant blooms, bronze-yellow. A mass of bloom in summer followed by continuous scattering of individual flowers.

Mermaid Repeat flowering. The large single, sulphur-yellow flowers open to reveal a mass of amber stamens which remain

Snake's head fritillary (*Fritillaria meleagris* 'Purple King'). *See page 52.*

after the petals have fallen off. The glossy foliage is unlike that of any other rose. Rampant on a south wall, less so on a north one where it will also grow well. (See page 93.)

New Dawn Repeat flowering. Pale flesh pink; very fragrant, the small- to medium-sized blooms are produced in clusters with great freedom.

Parkdirektor Riggers Repeat flowering. Brilliant deep crimson, semi-double blooms borne in large clusters, and set off by glossy dark green foliage.

Pink Perpétue Repeat flowering. Bright rose-pink with salmon-rose shading, medium sized double flowers in large clusters. Schoolgirl. Apricot-orange, highly scented flowers in small clusters.

Least trouble of all are the old rambler rose species – providing you have room for them. They are extremely vigorous, and once they have settled in will merrily ramble over unsightly sheds, up trees or over walls, with no attention at all, other than tying them up if necessary. Some of them have really huge heads of hundreds of flowers so tiny it is hard to believe they really are roses, though their scent gives them away. Most flower only once, but it is over a long period and a sight worth waiting for.

Short Selection

Filipes Kiftsgate Makes an enormous mound of interlacing shoots bearing most elegant, graceful foliage. At the beginning of July it is transformed into a giant's gyposophila, every side shoot becoming a fountain of hundreds of single flowers, each about $1\frac{1}{2}$ in across, with brilliant orange-yellow stamens and a powerful scent. In time it will grow to 30 ft high and wide. Dainty hips in the autumn.

Longicuspis Extra glossy leaves. Flowers later than other allied species. Multitudes of single white flowers with a rich banana fragrance for yards around. Followed by tiny red hips.

80

Bellflower, campanula (*C. persicifolia*). *See page 31.*

Very easy to establish, growing eventually to a height of 20 ft.

Rambling Rector A smother of semi-double white blooms, with a far-flung fragrance. 20 ft, excellent for hanging over hedges and stumps.

Wedding Day Similar to 'Rambling Rector' in size and behaviour, but with yellow pointed buds which open to white. The pointed petals give an unusual effect, and become spotted with pink when fading.

6 HEDGES

Hedges are what you make them. They can be created from any bushy plant or tree which happens to suit your purpose, from a bramble to a camellia. You may grow them for their looks – flowers, berries, coloured leaves – or for their usefulness. Whatever your reason, the easiest hedge will be one which needs the minimum amount of clipping and will grow in a variety of soils and situations.

Hedges can keep things both in and out . . . cigarette papers, noise, prying eyes, wind, if you are near a busy road, out; or children and pets, in. You may choose a hedge of flowers, berries, prickles, evergreen, see-through, natural or clipped. If noise is the main problem, then holly is the most soundproof.

Decide what height you want the hedge to be ultimately, then make up your mind whether you want a formal hedge for leaf only, or flowers and berries, evergreens, conifers, roses, bamboos . . . to name just a few choices.

Coloured foliage hedges are generally formal and cut closely with shears, while flowering and large-leaved evergreens are best pruned with secateurs. Unless you are a trimming addict, don't choose anything which has to be groomed more than once a year.

An evergreen hedge will give the maximum amount of protection from wind and noise, but is necessarily rather dull. A deciduous hedge will be easier to buy in the first place and also easier to establish. Whatever you choose, preparation of the soil before planting, is the same.

Preparing the soil

As an important and permanent part of the garden, the site for a hedge must be as carefully prepared as the foundations of a house. In early autumn dig the site as deeply as possible (about 2 ft) depending on soil conditions. Break up the lower earth and add drainage crocks or stones if necessary. Add as much organic matter as you can, mixed with the soil you have removed, and put it back to rest till spring. Then as the soil dries out, work in a dressing of a complete fertilizer at 2 oz a sq yd, then leave for another two weeks to settle before planting.

The spacing and planting times will depend on what you choose to grow, but in general, mid-March is best. Once planted, make sure the plants do not dry out, and in a dry spell you may need to water them twice a day. A thick mulch of peat afterwards will help to retain the moisture round.

Pruning

This naturally depends on what you grow, but need never be rigid. You can make your own rules to suit your needs and taste. *You* rule the hedge, it doesn't rule *you*. One firm 'don't'. Use secateurs not shears or clippers on broad-leaved evergreens. Butchered half-leaves are not a pretty sight and show their misery by turning brown.

Low-growing informal hedges, 3–4 ft

BERBERIS *thunbergii* Green leafed, and 'Atropurpurea', coppery-purple; best on lime-free soil. Fairly soon gets to 3 ft, and will continue to 4 or 5 ft but rather widespread. Lovely autumn colour, red-brown winter twigs. Deciduous. Clip in winter, and again in August if required. Plant 2 ft apart.

HYPERICUM *patulum* 'Hidcote' Semi-evergreen, large yellow flowers. Clip in spring. Plant 2 ft apart. (See opposite.)

POTENTILLA *farreri* Deciduous. Pure yellow flowers all summer, with dainty fern-like foliage. Prune in spring to shape and size you want.

Hypericum (*H. patulum 'Hidcote'*). See above.

PRUNUS *cistena* (crimson dwarf cherry) Single pink flowers and deep crimson foliage. The growing tips are bright blood red. Trim after flowering, and restrict annual increase in height to 6 in. Plant 2 ft apart.

Formal foliage hedges
BEECH Green-leaved beech quickly makes a good fairly compact hedge which can reach 5–10 ft. Good on chalk; avoid heavy wet soils. The rich brown leaves remain all winter till pushed off by the new growth in spring, like baby teeth. Plant 1 ft apart. Clip August–September. Greedy roots.

HORNBEAM Easier to establish on heavy soils than beech, which it resembles and has less greedy roots. Can stand exposed places and reach 5–8 ft. Plant 1½ ft apart. Trim in winter or late summer.

PRIVET, GOLDEN Less vigorous than the green. Needs good soil but less attention. 3–5 ft, plant 1½ ft apart.

Assorted hedges
COTONEASTER *simonsii* Erect semi-evergreen with colourful leaves and berries which draw attention to themselves after the leaves have fallen. Plant 1½ ft apart and trim in winter.

ILEX (holly) Common holly or its varieties make superb sound-proof hedges for sun or shade. They grow 6–10 ft and can be controlled by pruning (not clipping) in August. Slow growing, good for seaside but no use on chalk. The variegated kinds are equally good but slower in growth.

PRUNUS *laurocerasus* (common laurel) Large leaves, rapid growth for sun or shade. Does not like pure chalk. 6–10 ft. Prune in late summer. Evergreen.

Coniferous hedges (evergreen)
CHAMAECYPARIS *lawsoniana* 'Green Hedger' The best form of Lawson's cypress for hedging. Vigorous feathery, dark rich

86

green. Clip lightly in August–September. Grows to great height unless 'stopped'.

CUPRESSOCYPARIS *leylandii* Grey-green foliage, fast growing, 3 ft a year when settled in. Plant 2–3 ft apart and trim with secateurs in autumn.

TAXUS *baccata* (yew) Not so slow growing as is generally supposed. Creates dense formal hedges of any height. Good on chalk. Grows 1 ft a year once it gets going. Plant 2 ft apart. Clip in August–September.

Caution It is a mistake to allow hedge plants to increase too rapidly in height. During the formative years three or four clippings annually will be necessary to train them the way you want. When mature they will need the minimum attention.

Flowering and berrying hedges
These are mainly informal and should be planted 2–3 ft apart to allow them to spread naturally.

BERBERIS *darwinii* Rich orange yellow flowers April–May. Bluish purple berries; leaves like small shields. Prune foliage immediately aftet flowering. 4–6 ft. *B. stenophylla* has graceful, prickly arching sprays of small orange flowers in spring. 7–10 ft. Becomes dense.

COTONEASTER *lacteus* Olive-green leaves, milky-white flowers June, long-lasting red berries. Prune off long shoots in summer 8–10 ft.

ESCALLONIA Particularly good for sea districts. Prune after flowering to encourage a second flush of flowers. 5–6 ft. (See page 109.)

PRUNUS *pissardii nigra* (blaze) This popular prunus has deep purple foliage and pink flowers in spring. When the leaves fall in early December they disclose the deep purple of the wood. Trim in late March after flowering.

(*Above*) A recurrent-flowering rose for hedging (Blanc Double de Coubert).
(*Opposite*) For early summer flowering (*Rosa moyseii*). The flowers are followed
by these large, highly decorative hips. *See pages 91 and 98.*

PYRACANTHA *rogersiana* White flowers followed by masses of red berries. Prune in spring 4–6 ft.

SEA BUCKTHORN (*Hippophae rhamnoides*) Good for sea areas, 6–7 ft. Trim in spring. (See page 135.)

SYMPHORICARPOS (snowberry) Hybrid 'Erecta': magenta pink berries which last well. Trim in early spring 4–5 ft. *S.* 'White Hedge': masses of white berries, very compact. 4–5 ft.

TAMARIX *gallica* Resistant to sea winds with fine feathery flowers and foliage. Quick growing and good in all but the heaviest soils. Pink flowers, June–August 4–5 ft. Prune fairly hard in spring.

VIBURNUM *tinum* 'Eve Price' A fine form of the popular winter-flowering shrub laurustinus. The end of each shoot carries an umbel of pink-budded flowers turning to white. 6–8 ft.

Rose hedges

There is no clear distinction between shrub and hedging roses. All roses are shrubs. But some are more suitable for normal use than others. These form a mixed bag of many types . . . old roses; modern recurrent-flowering; floribundas; hybrid musks; hybrid rugosas; Chinensis; Bourbons, Gallicas and other groups.

According to your purpose, they can be trained on wires or ropes, or left to take their natural shape. Rose hedges are essentially informal compared with clipped hedges and pruning can be done to suit yourself and the type of hedge you want. To prevent bareness at the base, cut back some of the main growths to within about a foot of the ground from time to time in March.

Preparing the soil
This must be really well prepared as a hedge is usually

expected to be permanent. Dig the site thoroughly and incorporate as much manure or compost as you can afford, also chopped turf and bone meal before planting. You will get quicker and thicker results by planting them in a double, staggered row. Distances between plants will vary with the type of rose you choose.

Recurrent or intermittent flowering

Ballerina Delicate apple blossom pink with white eye. The small single flowers, displayed in large clusters, are fragrant and continue right through the summer, carried on vigorous growth. Foliage is glossy, light green and abundant. 3–4 ft.

Blanc Double de Coubert Pure white, with papery-textured petals, opening flat. The fragrant flowers are borne prolifically on a dense bush from 5–6 ft high. Very healthy, light green, deeply-veined foliage. (See page 88.)

Bonn Loosely semi-double flowers 3 in across in vivid coral-red shot with scarlet. Free flowering. Foliage light green, large and glossy. 5 ft by 4 ft.

Buff Beauty Buff or apricot-yellow, paling slightly with age. Fully double, sweetly scented and most prolific, especially late in the season. Handsome foliage on dark stems. 6 ft by 6 ft.

Chinatown Yellow, sometimes pink, full, 4 in across, fragrant. Very vigorous and tall, clothed with large, glossy, bright green leaves.

Cornelia Strawberry pink, yellow at base. Small rosette-like flowers with a musk scent. Glossy, small dark leaves, on graceful stems. Vigorous, 5–6 ft.

Dorothy Wheatcroft Bright orange-red with deeper shades, semi-double, 3 in across in huge trusses. Very vigorous, tall and branching with glossy foliage.

Elmsholm Light red or deep carmine pink, thinly-double

91

flowers in clusters very freely produced. Makes a bush about 5 ft high, with abundant reddish-green foliage. Keep an eye open for mildew.

Erfurt Citron-yellow, semi-double very large blooms edged with carmine. Very fragrant. Foliage bronze, wrinkled, leathery, vigorous and bushy. 5 ft.

Felicia Salmon-pink, shaded yellow. Perfectly formed buds, opening loosely. Very fragrant. Stiff, upright abundant growth and foliage, matt and medium green. 5 ft.

Frau Dagmar Hastrup Rose-pink, large single flowers continuously produced, followed by large crimson hips. Dark, crinkled foliage. 4 ft.

Gruss an Teplitz Deep scarlet with darker crayonings. Full, rounded, richly fragrant flowers. Dark green foliage, red when young. Vigorous growth, 6 ft.

Heidelberg Bright red, a little lighter on the reverse. Large, full flowers, carried freely in clusters, shapely at first, opening loosely. Abundant, glossy medium green foliage tinted bronze. Vigorous, 6 ft.

Honorine de Brabant Pale, lilac-pink, spotted and striped mauve and crimson. Flowers loosely formed, cupped and quartered. They have a refreshing, fruity scent and are borne recurrently on a strong bush up to 6 ft. Light green foliage.

Iceberg Pure white when open, pink tinged in bud, moderately full, 3 in across. Very free-flowering and slightly fragrant. Abundant dark green, glossy, pointed foliate. Growth: vigorous, tall and branching.

Kassel Deep scarlet, large semi-double flowers in small trusses. Dark, semi-glossy foliage carried on arching branches. Very vigorous and branching. 5–6 ft.

Lady Sonia Large, moderately full flowers, deep golden-

92

yellow, 4 in across, slightly fragrant, freely borne on upright growths, with ample dark green glossy foliage. 6–7 ft.

Moonlight Small semi-double flowers in clusters, pale lemon shading white, with musk scent. Small, glossy, dark green leaves, reddish-bronze when young, clothing dark brown wood. Vigorous growth, 6 ft.

Nymphenburg Pale salmon-pink with yellow base. Flowers large, fairly full and borne intermittently in small clusters. Sharp fruity scent. Foliage dark and glossy. Very vigorous to 6 ft.

Penelope Creamy salmon-pink, fading to off-white. The semi-double 3 in wide fragrant flowers are borne in clusters, with large heads of bloom in the autumn. Bronze-tinted semi-glossy foliage. Vigorous and spreading.

Prosperity White, tinted pink on petal edges. The many small petals from a round, pompon-like flower, $3\frac{1}{2}$ in across, borne in clusters. Glossy, dark green foliage, tinted bronze when young. Vigorous to 6 ft.

Queen Elizabeth Clear self-pink, moderately full blooms 4 in across. Slightly fragrant, free-flowering. Dark, glossy abundant foliage. Very vigorous, tall and upright, long almost thornless stems.

Sarah Van Fleet Bright rose-pink, large, semi-double, very fragrant flowers, produced freely in clusters. Large glossy medium green foliage, tinted bronze when young. Makes a dense bush up to 6 ft high.

Schneezwerg Pure white, rosette shaped semi-double blooms $2\frac{1}{2}$ in across. Flowers continuously with scarlet hips concurrently. Small, abundant foliage. Vigorous to 5 ft.

Shepherd's Delight Flame, orange and yellow, paler in autumn, semi-double, 3 in across, slightly fragrant, very free flowering. Very tall, vigorous and branching. Watch out for black spot.

Solus Orange-scarlet, semi-double $3\frac{1}{2}$in across, losing some brilliance with age and carried in small clusters on tall upright growth, with ample dark green glossy foliage.

Souvenir de la Malmaison Blush-white, large fragrant flowers, borne freely and recurrently on moderately bushy growth.

Sparrieshoop Large single salmon-pink flowers with yellow stamens. Fragrant. Free and continuous flowering. Vigorous growth to 6 ft with plentiful large, glossy, medium green foliage, coppery-bronze in the early stages.

Uncle Walter Scarlet, shaded crimson. Full, slightly fragrant blooms carried in clusters. Glossy, dark green foliage, crimson when young. Very vigorous, tall, upright.

Vanity Deep rose-pink, single, fragrant flowers, 3 in across, carried on strong growths. Very prolific in autumn. Growth vigorous and spreading, but rather sparse medium green foliage.

Wilhelm Rich crimson, semi-double blooms, $3\frac{1}{2}$in in large trusses. Slightly fragrant. Free and continuous flowering. Vigorous, branching 6 ft. Dark green, glossy, leathery foliage.

Will Scarlet Scarlet buds opening into semi-double scarlet flowers, paler in the centre. Dark green, bronze-tinted foliage. Makes a fine, moderately vigorous display on a 5 ft plant followed by orange-red hips.

Hedging roses for early summer flowering

This group has only one large flowering session, although a small quantity of flowers may be produced later in the season.

Canary Bird Rich yellow, single flowers opening to $2\frac{1}{2}$ in across and borne along the length of arching stems with brown wood. Very free flowering in May, followed by small, dark maroon hips. Eventually reaches 6 ft high, with bright green, small fern-like foliage.

Charles de Mills Purplish-crimson to maroon. Very large, full, quartered, fragrant blooms, on vigorous growths, up to 4 or 5 ft.

Conrad Ferdinand Meyer Silvery pink, very large and exceptionally full-petalled flowers with powerful scent, borne in May and June, and usually again in autumn. Very vigorous and rather gaunt with thorny stems, up to 8 ft.

Constance Spry Clear rose-pink. Large, fragrant, full cup-shaped flowers are borne all along the growths. Attractive pointed foliage, dark green, copper tinted when young. 6 ft.

Du Maître D'Ecole Soft old rose, shaded mauve and fading to lilac-pink. Full, large flowers, quartered, with button eyes, opening flat. Very fragrant. Growth is sturdy and vigorous with large leaves. 3 ft.

Fantin-Latour Large, fragrant, full, blush-pink flat flowers are borne in great profusion on a sturdy, bushy plant with large dark foliage. Up to 5 ft.

Fritz Nobis Flesh-pink, shaded salmon. Large, well-formed at first, opening semi-double. Very fragrant, followed by reddish hips. Growth is bushy and branching up to 6 ft, with glossy, medium green foliage. (See opposite.)

Frühlingsgold Large, clear yellow semi-single flowers, fading paler, carried on long arching branches. Very fragrant. Light green matt foliage and prickly wood.

Frühlingsmorgen Single deep pink flowers with yellow centre and maroon stamens. Small, matt medium green

An early summer flowering rose for hedging (Fritz Nobis). *See above.*

foliage. Usually produces some flowers after the early summer flush.

Gloire des Mousseaux Bright pink, fading a little with age. The flowers are large, quartered with button eyes, and light green mossing. A sturdy bush up to 4 ft with abundant light green foliage.

Lavender Lassie Lilac-pink, rosette-like flowers with many small musk-scented petals. Moderately vigorous, with glossy dark green foliage and some later blooms.

Mme Hardy Full, white-quartered flat flowers with a button eye, and exquisite scent. Vigorous growth to 5 ft, with abundant dark foliage.

Nuits de Young (Old Black) Deep maroon-purple with gold stamens. The flowers are small, well mossed and carried freely on a slender bush, 4–5 ft tall, with small, dark green foliage.

Rosa gallica (Rosa mundi) Crimson, semi-double flowers, splashed and striped with blush-pink and white. It makes a compact and dense bush up to 4 ft, exceptionally profuse during the early summer display.

R. moyseii Blood-red single flowers borne in small clusters, followed by highly decorative, large, bottle-shaped hips. Growth is tall, with thorny stems and small, dark green foliage. Up to 10 ft. (See page 89.)

R. primula (incense rose) Primrose yellow, single, fragrant flowers borne very freely in May, followed by small reddish hips. The young growth is reddish-brown, with small, dark green narrow leaves which diffuse the fragrance of myrrh. Upright, prickly growth up to 6 ft.

R. pteragonis cantabrigiensis Yellow, semi-single, fragrant and very free flowering in early summer, followed by small, orange-red hips. Very graceful fern-like foliage carried on hairy growths up to 7 ft.

R. rubrifolia Clear pink, single flowers, paling to white in the centre, followed by brownish-red hips. But the main attraction is the decorative growth, which is almost thornless, purplish-copper when young, with grey and mauve tinted foliage and a coppery sheen. Vigorous, open habit to 6 ft.

R. willmottiae Rich, mauve-pink single flowers, borne profusely on wiry, twiggy growth in early summer, followed by small pear-shaped orange-red hips. It forms a dense bush up to 6 ft or more high and wide, with very decorative small, fern-like glaucous leaves with 7 to 9 tiny leaflets, giving a light and dainty effect.

Scarlet Fire Bright scarlet single flowers, with gold stamens, borne freely in clusters along arching branches, and followed by large, pear-shaped red hips. Growth is vigorous and spreading, up to 6 ft high and wide, with dull green matt foliage.

Tour de Halakoff Cerise-magenta at first, veined and shaded purple, finally fading to lavender-grey. The large, full flowers are very fragrant but loosely formed, carried on vigorous but rather pendulous growth up to 6 ft, which, in well regimented gardens, may need some support.

William Lobb The colour varies from crimson-purple, to magenta, mauve and lilac-grey. Large, full, loosely-formed flowers with green moss, borne in large clusters on very vigorous growth up to 6 ft or more with prickly stems. Rather ungainly but full of character. Perhaps best planted with others of more graceful behaviour.

(*Above*) Kashmir mountain ash (*Sorbus cashmeriana*). An unusual, small, pink-flowered tree whose glistening white fruit often persists after the leaves have fallen. (*Opposite*) Weeping ash (*Fraxinus excelsior* 'Pendula'). *See page 113.*

7 TREES

Every garden of whatever size should have at least one tree to give it character and a sense of permanence. Initially, it will probably be the most expensive plant you put in it, though in time it will be the oldest and largest occupant. It is this permanence and eventual size in maturity which makes it essential to get the right tree in the right place for the right reason.

Decide first where the tree or trees are to go before you make your choice. Then ask the height and width it will ultimately become, and how many years it will take to do so.

Large types of trees should never be planted near a house. They have a more extensive root system than smaller growing ones and are best suited for woodlands. Position them where they will not shade windows, borders of hardy perennials or rock gardens. Keep them away from buildings to avoid damage to foundations, or clogging of gutters. You will appreciate them better from a distance.

Avoid planting too close to the boundaries of your garden where it can become a nuisance to neighbours, or passers-by if it overhangs a pavement. Think ahead to what kind of mopping-up operations may be necessary in the autumn, in the way of dropped leaves, berries or fruit – horse chestnuts for example.

Something you like in a neighbouring garden is not necessarily going to be right for yours. The scale and shape may not be alike. Perhaps a tall thin tree could be fitted in where one with a lovely rounded head would have to be constantly chopped about to keep it within bounds. It is reckoned that in ten years, a tree will increase the size of its head of branches to about four times what it was at the time of planting. Lawn grass is not too happy in dense shade or with soggy masses of leaves left on it.

When choosing, consider what characteristics are most important to you. Shape: narrowly upright, round-headed or weeping. Foliage: deciduous or evergreen; large leaves or small; dense or open; spring, summer and autumn colouring (silver, gold and purple summer foliage helps to create interest and contrasts with the trees which have only green foliage). Do you want blossom, followed by decorative or edible fruit? Coloured or strangely marked bark?

Put these considerations beside your reasons for wanting a tree at all . . . for shade, shelter, as a windscreen, to soften outlines, add height, entirely for the pleasure of looking at it; and you should be able to narrow the field from the bewildering choice that is offered.

By planting trees on the northern or western side of your garden you can minimize the loss of sunlight and avoid large parts of the garden being in shadow, except for a short period. Make sure you will not be cutting your neighbours off from the sunshine at some later date.

When in doubt, choose a standard tree for a smallish garden. That is one which comes with a single 5–6 ft clear trunk, from the top of which the head of branches will form. You get the effect of it almost as soon as it is planted and there will be room to get under and around it to mow the grass or hoe down the weeds.

Planting

Hardy trees are surprisingly tolerant of soil conditions, provided drainage is good. Many come from the mountains where soil is not deep except in the river valleys. The limiting factor for a number of species is the amount of lime present. Many trees growing naturally on acid or neutral soils will grow equally well on soils with a moderate lime content, particularly if the soil is deep and fertile. In general, conifers prefer acid or neutral soils, while malus (apples), prunus (cherries, plums, peaches, almonds, etc.), pyrus (pears), crataegus (thorns) and sorbus (rowans and service trees), prefer alkaline soils.

It is curious that most of the lime-loving plants will grow well in neutral and acid soils; the calcifuge (lime haters) cannot adapt themselves, and turn up their toes in any soil containing lime.

Prepare the spot where a tree is to go before it arrives. Dig a hole larger than the span of the roots and loosen the soil in the bottom. Drive in a stake and place the tree at the depth it grew · in the nursery. Add moistened peat and two handfuls of bone meal in returning the soil and firming it round the roots. Give the trunk a shake or two up and down to make sure there are no air pockets and finally tread round with the heel. Secure the tree to the stake with inch-wide plastic or rubber tree ties, one at the top and one halfway down.

The usual planting time is from November to March when the ground is not water-logged or frozen. Evergreens are best planted in September or April, but may also be planted during the winter season. So many plants are now grown in containers, it is possible to plant them at all times of the year, provided you are prepared to give them special watering attention, and protection from cold winds if necessary.

Ask for advice when you buy them if in any doubt.

Special purpose trees

Here is a short guide to help you choose trees for a particular purpose. For a detailed list of easy-to-grow suitable trees, see page 108.

SMALL SPECIMEN TREES
Acer negundo
Amelanchier
Betula pendula 'Youngii'
Cotoneaster pendula
Crataegus (hawthorn)
Laburnum
Magnolia
Malus (flowering crab)

Vine (*Vitis coignetiae*). Richest of the ornamental vines. *See page 73.*

Prunus (flowering cherry)
Pyrus salicifolia 'Pendula'
Robinia fastigiata
Salix purpurea 'Pendula'
Sorbus (See page 100.)
Ulmus glabra 'Camperdownii'

WEEPING TREES

Alnus incana 'Pendula' (weeping alder)
Betula pendula 'Youngii' (Young's weeping silver birch)
Buxus sempervirens 'Pendula' (weeping form of common box)
Crataegus monogyma 'Pendula' (weeping hawthorn; *rosea* has pink flowers)
Cotoneaster hybridus 'Pendulus' (weeping cotoneaster)
Fraxinus excelsior 'Pendula' (weeping ash; see page 101)
Ilex aquifolium 'Argenteo-Marginata, Pendula' (Perry's silver weeping holly)
Laburnum anagyroides 'Pendulum' (graceful weeping laburnum)
Malus (crab-apples with pendulous branches)
M. floribunda 'Excellens Thiel' (crimson buds, pink flowers, no fruit)
M. prunifolia 'Pendula' (weeping Siberian crab, small scarlet persistent fruit)
M. pumila pendula 'Elise Rathke' (weeping native crab)
Prunus kiku shidare 'Zakura' (Cheal's weeping cherry)
P. Persica 'Windle Weeping' (weeping peach with double pink flowers)
P. subhirtella 'Pendula' (weeping rosebud cherry)
Pyrus salicifolia 'Pendula' (weeping silver willow-leaved pear)
Salix 'vitellina Aurea Pendula' (golden weeping willow)
Salix purpurea 'Pendula' (weeping purple willow - keeps modest proportions)
Sorbus aria (weeping form of whitebeam)
Ulmus glabra 'camperdownii (weeping wych elm)

TREES FOR BARK EFFECT

Acer griseum (paperbark maple; also snake bark varieties)
Betula (most birches)
Fraxinus 'Aurea' ('golden barked ash')

106

Prunus serrula 'Tibetica'
Salix alba 'Chermesina'
S. alba 'Tristis'
S. alba 'Vitellina'
S. daphnoides acutifolia
S. purpurea 'Pendula'
Tilia platyphyllos 'Rubra'

DEFENSIVE TREES FOR THE SEASIDE
Acer pseudoplatanus (sycamore)
Crataegus (hawthorn)
Populus alba (white poplar) ·
Quercus ilex (evergreen or holm oak)
Salix (willow)
Sorbus aria (whitebeam)
Sorbus intermedia (Swedish whitebeam)

TREES FOR DAMP PLACES
Alnus (alders)
Betula nigra (river birch)
Betula pendula (alba verrucosa) (silver birch)
Crataegus oxycantha (common hawthorn)
Populus (poplars)
Salix (willows)
Sorbus aucuparia varieties (mountain ash or rowan)

SMALL TREES FOR SMALL GARDENS

Standard trees

Amelanchier canadensis (white flowers, brilliant autumn foliage, 12 ft)
Acer griseum (cinnamon-barked maple, brilliant autumn foliage, 20 ft)
Catalpa bignonioides 'Aurea' (golden Indian bean tree, 10 ft)
Crataegus carrieri (ornamental thorn, orange berries, 12 ft)
Koelreuteria paniculata (Orange-yellow flowers followed by bladder fruit; the true 'willow pattern' leaves, 10 ft)
Laburnum alpinum (yellow flowers, 12 ft)
Malus 'Profusion' (wine-red flowers, 15 ft)

Prunus persica 'Clara Meyer' (double pink flowering peach, 12 ft)

Prunus Amanogawa 'Lombardy Poplar Cherry' (pink flowers, 15 ft)

Prunus blireiana (pale pink early plum, 12 ft)

Prunus okame (pink early flowering cherry, 15 ft)

Sorbus vilmorinii (red-berried mountain ash, brilliant autumn foliage)

Conifers

Chamaecyparis lawsoniana (Lawson's cypress) 'Allumii' (bluish-grey foliage, 10 ft)

C. lawsoniana 'Ellwoodii' (silvery-blue foliage, 6 ft)

C. lawsoniana 'Fletcheri' (silvery-blue foliage, 9 ft)

C. lawsoniana 'Pottenii' (bright green, 9 ft)

Juniperus communis 'Hibernica' (Irish juniper, greyish foliage, 6 ft)

Taxus baccata 'Fastigiata' (upright Irish yew, 8 ft)

Easily grown and accommodated trees

ACER The maples are widely varying foliage trees, ideal for modern gardens because they provide interest through all the seasons. All thrive in moist, but not wet soils.

A. pseudoplatanus (common sycamore) Not for small gardens. Invaluable quick grower for coastal or exposed sites. 25 ft.

A. pseudoplatanus 'Brilliantissimum' Lovely in spring, the leaves salmon-pink when unfolding, later streaked with gold, turning finally to green. 10–15 ft.

A. griseum Gloriously coloured red and scarlet leaves in autumn. Old bark peels to show cinnamon coloured under-bark. 12–15 ft.

'Snake-Bark' varieties

A. hersii (*grosseri hersii*) The young wood is red, the older wood red striped yellowish green. Broad, round-headed, 15–20 ft.

Escallonia (*E.* 'G.F. Ball'). Another possibility for a flowering hedge. *See page 87.*

A. henryi The bluish green bark is very striking, as are the young bronzy red shoots and leaves.

A. pennsylvanicum Makes a perfectly shaped tree, and has conspicuous white striped bark. Good autumn colour. 20 ft.

A. negundo 'Auratum' Bright golden yellow leaves. 20 ft.

A. negundo 'Variegata'. One of the most effective foliage trees. The light green leaves have silver variegation. Round-headed, always cheerful to see. 15–20 ft.

AMELANCHIER *canadensis* (snowy Mespilus) Attractive at various stages. White flowers appear in April when the half-open leaves are tinged pink. Crimson fruit ripens in June and the foliage colours richly in autumn. Round-headed, 12–18 ft.

ALNUS *incana* (grey alder) Very hardy, particularly for cold wet sites.

A. incana 'Aurea' Young shoots and foliage are yellow, catkins conspicuously red-tinted. Bright orange wood in winter. 15–20 ft.

A. incana 'Pendula' Lovely in January with bright catkins. Makes a handsome weeping specimen. Grey-green leaves, 25 ft.

BETULA (birch) Shallow rooted, so take care when underplanting with bulbs, etc.

B. pendula (*alba verrucosa*) ('the queen of the woods', our native silver birch) Graceful pendulous young branches. White peeling bark develops with age. 25 ft. Not fussy about soil.

B. nigra (river birch) A pyramidal tree noted for its shaggy blackish bark. Soft green leaves. Thrives in wet sites. 25 ft.

B. pendula 'Youngii' (Young's weeping birch) Forms dome-shaped weeping trees with branches reaching to the ground. Ideal in small gardens. 12–15 ft.

BUXUS *sempervirens* 'Aurea Pendula' (golden weeping box) Branches drooping, leaves variegated with gold. Thrives in any soil, sun or shade.

CATALPA *bignonioides* The large ovate fresh green leaves form a backcloth to upright spikes of white flowers flecked yellow and purple; July–August. These resemble horse chestnut candles. Long 'runner beans' form in autumn. Needs good moist soil and sun. Forms a wide, rounded head. 15 ft.

C. bignonioides 'Aurea' The golden form with large gleaming yellow leaves unfurling in May and retaining their freshness throughout the summer.

COTONEASTER The answer for anyone wanting an evergreen standard tree. Adaptable and especially good as specimens and as screens when planted 10–12 ft apart. All have white or pink tinted flowers in May–June. Sizes from 8–15 ft.

C. 'Cornubia' Deep green evergreen leaves, flat heads of white flowers in May, cascades of large scarlet berries in autumn. Broad flat-headed, 15 ft.

C. hybridus 'Pendulus'. One of the few evergreen weepers. Exceptionally effective, the pendulous branches festooned in autumn with large red berries. Rarely exceeds 8 ft.

C. rothschildianus The light green, willow-like leaves always look fresh and in autumn provide a captivating backcloth for the yellow berries. These ripen late and last well into the winter, as the birds usually leave them alone, preferring red ones. Round-headed, 12–15 ft.

CRATAEGUS The hawthorns are the last of the spring flowering trees. They thrive anywhere.

C. carrierei One of the best since not only do the large orange berries last long, but the large oval leaves turn a bright orange colour before they fall in autumn. White flowers 1 in across. Sturdy upright tree, 12–15 ft.

C. prunifolia Polished dark green, broad oval leaves, which turn brilliant tones of orange and scarlet in autumn before the rich crimson fruit colours. White flowers in June in 3 in wide clusters. Round, 15 ft.

C. monogyma 'Pendula' (weeping thorn) A form with graceful arching branches and white flowers. 'Pendula Rosea' has pink flowers.

CHAMAECYPARIS LAWSONIANA (Lawson's cypress) This tall pyramidal tree is one of the most useful and ornamental of all conifers. The typical form makes an excellent tall screen and can be planted in exposed positions or in shade. The named varieties vary from dwarf plants for the rock garden to tall stately specimens in many shades of green, blue, yellow and silver.

C. lawsoniana 'Ellwoodii' A charming slow-growing variety with erect branches densely covered with feathery, glaucous-blue foliage. Eventually attains a height of 6–9 ft.

C. lawsoniana 'Fletcheri' A very popular slow-growing variety, forming close, glaucous-blue feathery pyramids. 9–15 ft.

C. lawsoniana 'Pottenii' Beautiful slow-growing conical form, with feathery sea-green foliage. 9 ft.

FRAXINUS (ash) Growing in almost any site, including wet soils by rivers etc., they stand shade when young.

F. excelsior 'Aurea' (golden barked ash) The yellow of the wood is outstanding in winter. The leaves are soft yellow at first, turn green, then a clear yellow in autumn. 15 ft.

F. excelsior 'Pendula' (weeping ash) Spreading, pendulous branches well clothed in elegant pinnate foliage. (See page 101.)

ILEX (holly) Thrives in almost any well-drained soil, in full or semi-shade as well as sun. If the leaves drop after transplanting, this is an indication that the plant will live.

Strawberry tree (*Arbutus unedo*). *See page 147.*

I. aquifolium 'Argento-marginata Pendula' (Perry's silver weeping holly) It berries freely.

JUNIPERUS They are among the most suitable conifers for calcareous soils, though this is not essential for their well-being. Tough and hardy and tolerant of most conditions.

J. communis 'Hibernica' (Irish juniper) A close-growing, columnar variety, suitable for formal gardens. (See page 119.)

KOELREUTERIA *paniculata*. A beautiful late flowering tree with pinnate 'willow pattern' leaves, reddish in spring, and yellow in autumn. The upright 15-in-high yellow flower panicles in July–August are followed by bronze, bladder-like fruits. A slow grower worth waiting for. Any soil, full sun. 15 ft.

LABURNUM ('golden rain') There are few more attractive trees flowering May–June which are suitable for small gardens. Graceful in habit with pendulous flowering twigs. The subsequent brown pods contain black poisonous seeds.

L. anagyroides 'Pendulum' A low-growing, elegant tree, with long slender drooping branches.

L. alpinum 'Pendulum' Very slow-growing form developing a low, dome-shaped head of stiffly weeping branches.

L. alpinum 'Pyramidale'. A form with erect branches.

L. alpinum (Scotch laburnum) A small, broad-headed tree producing extra long, drooping racemes of fragrant flowers in early June. Glossy foliage, deep shining green above, pale and slightly hairy beneath.

MAGNOLIA Several kinds grow into standard trees as distinct from the big bush form in which this plant is more often seen.

M. kobus Very hardy small Japanese tree, excellent for all types of soils, including chalky. It grows an airy 15 ft. Easy, but you must wait till it is 12–15 years old before it produces

114   Tree hollyhock (*Hibiscus syriacus*). *See page 149.*

fragrant white flowers. They are then regularly borne with majestic freedom during April.

M. soulangeana 'Picture' A slender vigorous, erect and narrow 12 ft. It flowers when quite young. Large leaves and long, erect flowers, purple outside, white inside. Both these magnolias grow in any soil and like a sunny position, but when they are out of flower they can be as dull as syringa (lilac) so try and make use of them as boundary screens.

MALUS The red-flowering crabs provide a colour not found in the cherries and the pale pink varieties have a pure freshness not seen in the rival genus. The ornamental fruit is invaluable, and on heavy land the crabs are more reliable than cherries.

M. floribunda (Japanese crab) Deep red in bud, opening pale pink and turning white. April. 12 ft. Small fruits of red and yellow.

M. 'Profusion' Outstanding, flowers in great profusion, wine-red, slightly fragrant about $1\frac{1}{2}$ in across, borne in clusters of six or seven in April. 15–20 ft. Fruits small, ox-blood red. Young leaves coppery-crimson.

M. tschonoskii Strong, erect and slender, up to 30 ft. Flowers white, tinged pink; fruits, yellowish-green tinged reddish-purple. One of the best trees for autumn colour with its bold foliage of yellow, orange, purple and scarlet.

PRUNUS Very free-flowering genus which included ornamental almonds, peaches, plums, sloes and cherries. The most valuable of the spring-flowering trees for gardens of all sizes. It is essential to prepare the ground thoroughly and make sure it is well drained. The whole group benefits from lime. No pruning is needed, but any unwanted branches should be removed immediately after flowering.

P. serrulata (hybrid Japanese cherries) *erecta* ('Amanogowa'). Beautiful semi-double, scented soft pink clusters of flowers enshrine the stem which becomes a pillar of flower in April–May. It has the habit of Lombardy poplar but only 15–20 ft.

116

Excellent for limited spaces and good autumn colour.

P. blireiana (flowering plum) Delightful early-flowering (March) tree with coppery foliage and masses of double pink rosette-like flowers produced on the bare stems. Broadly rounded and twiggy, 15–18 ft.

P. 'Okame' (flowering cherry) A delightful small tree at any time. One of the earliest to flower, it produces dainty rose pink tubular flowers on the leafless slender branches in March–April. The small, pretty leaves are bronze when young. 15–18 ft.

P. pendula rosea (Cheal's Weeping; or 'Kiku Shidare Zakura') The long branches sweep down to the ground and in April are clothed with clusters of pink buds, then double bright pink flowers.

P. subhirtella 'Pendula Rubra' Charming weeper with pendulous slender branches bedecked with dainty deep rose single flowers in April.

P. serrula 'Tibetica' Small but vigorous tree whose main attraction is the glistening surface of its polished red-brown, mahogany-like new bark. Leaves are narrow and willow-like. Small white flowers are produced with the foliage in late April.

PYRUS *salicifolia* 'Pendula' Beautiful silver-leaved weeping form of the 'willow leaf pear'. Leaves are covered with silky down until early summer when they turn grey-green. It comes into leaf early and waits till November before it drops its foliage for winter. The white flowers in April are of no account. It is at its best planted as a focal point. About 15 ft.

QUERCUS *ilex* (evergreen or holm oak) Deep-rooted but not fussy about site. A stately evergreen forming a dense rounded crown. The unfolding leaves are covered with hairs giving the tree an ochre-green to grey-yellow appearance. Can take some clipping. Slow starter but will reach 20 ft when established.

SALIX (willows) The willows provide colour and interest early

(*Above*) Mountain ash, rowan (*Sorbus aucuparia*) and (*opposite*) juniper (*Juniperus communis* 'Hibernica'). *See pages 120 and 114.*

when little else is stirring. There are varieties suitable for any and every site. Most are fast growers particularly in their youth, but can easily be controlled by drastic pruning if necessary.

S. alba 'Tristis' (golden weeping willow; also known by various other names) The most frequent victim of ill-considered planting. Beautiful, but keep it well away from buildings. The roots need moisture and will break into drains to find it.

S. purpurea 'Pendula' (American weeping willow) Much less rampant than the golden forms. Ideal for small gardens, forming a graceful umbrella of shoots covered with purple bark and long glaucous foliage. 12–15 ft.

SORBUS *aucuparia* 'Pyrus' (mountain ash or rowan) A round-headed tree with smooth, silvery-grey bark. Orange red berries. 15 ft. (See page 118.)

S. aria (whitebeam) Small to medium size native tree with compact, usually rounded head of branches. Oval greyish-white leaves at first which later turn bright green above and vivid white below. They turn again in autumn to gold and russet, when the bunches of deep crimson fruits can be seen at their best. One of the best trees for windswept and seaside districts and industrial areas. There are many varieties to choose from.

S. intermedia (Swedish whitebeam) Round-headed tree valuable for exposed sites, medium sized and dense. Grey-white, deeply lobed leaves with yellowish-grey down beneath. White flowers in large heads. Bright red fruits. May ultimately reach 20 ft.

S. essertauiana Has the best autumn leaf colour. The large leaflets unfold in mid-March – early April, a rich copper colour with a silvery sheen from the grey down. They are green until late autumn when they turn bronze. The heavily scented flowers are followed by late ripening, brilliant red berries which are usually completely ignored by the birds.

S. hupehensis Grey-green foliage turns red in autumn. The

120

berries stay on the trees like pale pink marbles well into winter and are absolutely bird-proof. Narrow growing, 15 ft.

S. vilmorinii (red-berried mountain ash) Quickly makes a round-headed 12 ft tree with white flowers in late spring followed by pinkish white berries in early autumn.

TILIA *platyphyllos* 'Rubra' (red twigged lime) This is much superior to the common lime. The red branches are outstanding in winter. It will stand 'pollarding'. 25 ft.

ULMUS *glabra camperdownii* 'Pendula' (the umbrella-shaped weeping elm) A beautiful lawn tree. The pale yellow-green bract-like seeds in April are most attractive. 14–16 ft.

8 GROUND COVER PLANTS

Ground cover plants must be treated with caution. They have the unfortunate knack of smothering or strangling any cultivated treasures which get in their way. Told to get on with the job, they are not selective. Some are invasive with roots that spread underground. Others run over the ground, but are easily removed. The safest ground cover plants are those which make dense clumps.

If you have a new garden you will find some of the following plants invaluable for keeping the ground free of annual weeds and at the same time providing colour and interest.

They can be planted around young shrubs and trees, well away from the roots, and as the larger shrubs increase in spread, the ground cover plants can be moved to fresh areas, gradually bringing the whole garden under control with the minimum of cultivation.

It is useless to expect ground cover plants to smother established perennial weeds. You must start with clean, well dug, fertile ground. The term ground cover plants embraces a large and varied assortment. They may be shrubs, perennials, foliage plants, evergreens, flowerers, creepers, climbers (for covering banks), from tiny ground-hugging alpines to quite tall plants of 3–4 ft. They need a variety of soils and situations. As with all garden planting, take your time, keep the ground weed free while you decide what you like best of the plants capable of doing what you ask of them.

Brunnera (*B. macrophylla*). A clump-forming hardy plant to use as ground cover. *See page 132.*

Low growing carpeting plants

The following are those suitable for special purposes and positions.

For dry shade

AJUGA *reptans* 'Multicolor' Bugles 6 in, variegated bronze foliage, blue flowers.

ASARUM (wild ginger) Red flowers, 3 in.

CONVALLARIA (lily of the valley) 4–6 in.

IVIES, trailing.

SAXIFRAGA *umbrosa* 'Variegata' (variegated London pride) 6 in.

VINCA (periwinkles) 6 9 in.

For moist shade

COTYLEDON *oppositifolia* Golden flowers in chains. 4 in.

CYCLAMEN, DWARF Pink and white. 3 in.

HOUSTONIA *caerula* 'Fred Millard' Blue, 3 in.

LYSIMACHIA *nummularia* 'Aurea' (creeping Jenny) Golden flowers and foliage, 6 in.

LAMIUM *galeobdolon* 'Variegatum' Gold leaved variegations, vigorous, 1 ft.

NEPETA *hederacea* 'Variegata' (catmint) Trailing variegated foliage, blue flowers.

OMPHALODES *verna* Bright blue, 6 in.

For hot, dry, sunny banks

ACAENA Red burrs, bronze-green leaves, 2 in.

ALYSSUMS Gold or yellow flowers, 2–6 in.

HELIANTHEMUMS (rock roses) Various colours, 9 in.

HELICHRYSUMS (carpeting forms) Silver leaves, 6 in.

LAMIUM *maculatum* 'Roseum' Pink, green and white leaves, 4 in.

RAOULIAS Silver leaved, $\frac{1}{2}$ in.

SEDUMS Various heights and colours, usually yellow, red or white. (See page 127.)

SEMPERVIVUMS (houseleeks) Various colours, from 2 in.

THYMES (especially *T. serpyllum*) Creeping.

With coloured foliage

AJUGA *reptans* 'Atropurpurea' Bronze purple, 6 in.

CALLUNA *vulgaris* 'Aurea' Soft yellow, 12 in.

LYSIMACHIA *nummularia* 'Aurea' Gold, 3 in.

NEPETA *hederacea* 'Variegata' White or pink margins, 1–2 in.

VINCA *minor* 'Aureo-variegata' Leaves spotted with yellow, 8 in.

Evergreen carpeters

ARCTOSTAPHYLOS *californica* and *myrtifolia* Pink flowers, red berries, trailing.

AUBRIETAS Mauves, blues and reddish purple, creeping.

ERICA *carnea* (heathers) Reds and whites, 6–12 in or more.

HEDERA *helix* (ivy) Various creeping varieties.

HYPERICUM *calycinum* (rose of Sharon) Golden, large-flowered, 1 ft.

IBERIS *sempervirens* (perennial candytuft) White in spring, 9 in.

JUNIPERUS *horizontalis* Blue foliaged conifer and *J. sabina* 'Tamaricifolia', blue-green, 12 in.

PACHYSANDRA *terminalis* Greenish-white flowers. 9 in.

THYMUS *drucei* Forms miniature lawns like patchwork quilts.

VINCA *minor*.

Surface spreading plants

The following ground-cover plants spread over the surface of the soil:

DICENTRA *formosa* 'Elba' White dainty locket-shaped flowers,

125

almost continuously in bloom, pale green ferny leaves, 18 in.

EPIMEDIUM (berberis family) Prefers shade but will grow almost anywhere. Long-stalked divided leaves. Tiny columbine-like flowers are borne on wiry stems. One of the most beautiful spring flowers.

GERANIUM (cranesbill) These are indispensable for this purpose. Easy to cultivate in any reasonably well-drained soil, sun or shade. All are weed smotherers. *G. macrorrhizum* is the best colonizer. Divided, light green, fragrant leaves. Soft pink flowers. 1 ft by 1 ft. Though a spreader, is never a weed. Some autumn colour.

LAMIUM *galeobdolon* 'Variegatum' (dead-nettle family) Not to be considered in restricted spaces; it spreads at alarming speed. Evergreen marbled leaves. Spikes of soft yellow dead-nettle flowers in spring. 1 ft. Likes shade.

L. maculatum Not as invasive as the above. 6 in, leaves sage green striped with white. Will grow anywhere.

ORIGANUM *vulgare* 'Aureum' (common marjoram) The aromatic leaves are used in cooking. Forms a mat of small leaves, brilliant yellow until summer when they turn green. 1 ft.

OXALIS *oregana* (wood-sorrel family) Large clover leaves, light green preceded by coppery pink trumpet flowers, 5 in. Grows rapidly.

POLYGONUM *affine* (dock family) Easily grown in sun or shade where soil does not dry out. Dense, narrow leaves 4 in. high which turn rich brown in winter. Flowers pink, 1 ft.

SAXIFRAGA *umbrosa* (London pride). Rosettes of attractive green, knitting together in an excellent net. Dainty spires of tiny flowers make a foam of pink in April–May. 1 ft.

STACHYS *lanata* 'Silver Carpet' A mass of silver-grey evergreen

The sedum family is useful as ground cover
(*S. cauticola*). See pages 39, 44 and 125.

woolly leaves. A new, non-flowering form of 'lamb's ears'.

S. macrantha A Caucasian plant making a mat of good leaves, with erect stems bearing whorls of hooded rosy-mauve blooms in summer. 2 ft. Especially good as carpets for 'old' roses.

SYMPHYTUM *grandiflorum* (borage family; comfrey) Weed-proof carpet for cool shady places in any soil. Evergreen. The cream tubular flowers tipped red in bud are beautiful in spring. 1 ft.

TIARELLA *cordifolia* The dense mass of heart-shaped leaves excludes all weeds. Innumerable spikes of white flowers like small bottle-brushes. A merry plant. 9 in.

VIOLA 'Huntercombe Purple' Intense royal purple violet. Protect from hottest sun. Any fertile soil. 6 in.

Underground spreading plants
The following ground-cover plants spread with underground shoots:

ACANTHUS *spinosus* Superb stately sun lovers for any soil. 4–5 ft. Large dark green leaves about 2 ft, deeply divided with spiny points, arching and handsome. The spires of soft mauve foxglove-like flowers are striking and turn into magnificent seed heads.

ANEMONE *vitifolia* 'Robustissima' Vigorous colonizer. Handsome leafy plant with quantities of silvery pink flowers. 3 ft.

ASARUM *europaeum* Round, glossy, evergreen leaves, 4 ft. Flowers insignificant. Grows best in heavy soil and cool positions.

ASPERULA *odorata* (woodruff) Heads of pure white stars in April and May, 6 in. Prized for its smell of new-mown hay when dried. Prefers shade in any soil.

CENTAUREA *dealbata* 'Steenbergii' (daisy family) Pretty feathery

128

foliate. Rich lilac-purple flowers on strong stems. 18 in. Sun-loving. Heavy or light well-drained soil.

CERATOSTIGMA *plumbaginoides* Invasive roots, creating a dense mass of dark foliage, turning to brilliant colour in autumn when the heads of deep blue flowers appear. 1 ft. Any fertile soil in full sun.

CONVALLARIA *majalis* (lily of the valley) Best under trees or shrubs. Long-lasting leaves with exquisitely scented flowers. Grows where it likes but not always where it is planted. Try it in a variety of places. Semi-shade, any soil.

EUPHORBIA *robbiae* (spurge family) Easy in sun or part shade, well-drained fertile soil. Evergreen rosettes of broad dark leaves. Elegant heads of yellow-green in spring. 2 ft. Very striking.

POLYGONATUM *multiflorum* (Solomon's seal) A gracious shade-loving plant for under trees or against a north wall. Any soil. The arching stems bear broad leaves, and bells of greeny white in clusters. 2–3 ft.

POLYGONUM *affine* 'Donald Lowndes'. Thick compact spikes of pink flowers, 1 ft, with dense narrow leaves 4 in high which turn rich brown in winter.

P. amplexicaule 'Atrosanguineum' Easy in sun or shade where soil does not dry out. Beautiful from end of June until frosts in autumn. A big leafy clump, 4 ft, slowly increasing in size. Innumerable erect spikes of flowers like spikes of lavender, but rich crimson.

P. campanulatum Never-ending display of small pink flowers in branching heads, from mid-summer onwards. Prefers moist or cool soil in partial shade. Stout colonizing plant. 3 ft.

TRACHYSTEMON (borage family) Thrives in moist or dry soils, sun or shade. Great, hairy, aspidistra-like leaves smother the

129

ground, but before they emerge the branching flower stems arise, holding starry blue flowers. 2 ft. For large rough areas.

Large clump formers for moist ground
ASTILBES Large choice, all form weed-proof ground-cover. Ferny leaves. The seed heads of rich brown remain erect during winter. 2–3 ft.

FILIPENDULAS *purpurea* Fine large leaves, leafy stem crowned by a flat head of cerise-crimson. 4 ft.

LIGULARIA *clivorum* 'Desdemona' Vivid orange daisies on branching stems. In striking contrast with the large leaves which are dark mahogany-brown on top and gorgeous red-brown beneath. 4 ft.

LYSICHITUM *americanum* Handsome 1 ft high, yellow arum flowers arise from the bare soil in early spring, followed by enormous paddle-shaped leaves 4 ft long and 1 ft wide, which remain beautiful till the autumn. Ideal for smothering weeds in boggy soil. Must be very wet the year round. (See page 131.)

PELTIPHYLLUM *peltatum* Immense, nearly circular leaves on stout stems, burnished in sun in late summer. The pink starry flowers on strong hairy stems appear in early spring before the leaves. 3 ft. Good for the side of a pond or stream where its thick iris-like roots prevent erosion. Plant as for irises, with the top of the rhizome root exposed.

PRIMULA *florindae* (Himalayan cowslip) Big rounded leaves; several stems arise when established, bearing drooping heads of clear yellow fragrant bells powdered white. Long flowering period. 2 ft.

RODGERSIA *podophylla* Smooth, bronze, circular leaves divided into broad jagged lobes. Cream flowers in a fluffy spike. Leaves colour best in full sun. Needs rich, deep, moist soil. Slow spreader.

130

Lysichitum (*L. americanum*). A handsome plant for boggy places. *See above.*

Clump-forming hardy plants

The following can be used as ground cover when planted in groups.

ALCHEMILLA *alpina* Forms a mat of divided leaves, over which are borne short sprays of pale green, insignificant flowers. The shining silvery texture of the undersides of the leaves is like the finest satin. 5 in.

A. mollis Downy, rounded leaves, and an airy display of tiny greeny yellow stars in feathery sprays, 18 in high, which remain beautiful for a long period.

ALYSSUM *saxatile* Fluffy heads of brilliant yellow. 10 in.

ANAPHALIS *nubigena* (daisy family) Easy about type of soil but flags if too dry in summer. 8 in.

ARTEMISIA *absinthium* Elegant silver filigree foliage and graceful spires of tiny silver bobbles. 3 ft.

ASTER Dwarf hybrid Michaelmas daisies. 10–15 in.

BERGENIA Slowly creeping root; great round, shining, leathery green leaves. Many assume burnished tones and retain them through the winter, turning green in spring. Strong red stems bear dense heads of magenta-pink flowers in spring. They grow in any soil, sun or shade but colour best in sun. They look particularly good against paving.

BRUNNERA *macrophylla* Vivid forget-me-not flowers are borne on 18-in stems in April–May. Large heart-shaped leaves create attractive greenery through the summer. Any fertile soil. Prefers some moisture and half or full shade. (See page 123.)

CALTHA *palustris* (kingcup or marsh marigold) Double ranunculus-like golden flowers contrast with glossy rounded leaves which later create handsome ground cover. Needs moist soil.

CRAMBE *cordifolia* Enormous, deeply-lobed leaves above which

132

arises a huge gypsophila-cloud of small white stars. 6 ft. Full sun, well-drained soil, thrives on lime.

EUPHORBIA *polychroma* (spurge). Flat heads of greeny yellow bracts and flowers. 1 ft.

HELLEBORUS *corsicus* Bushy plant with beautiful divided, hand-like grey-green leaves and clusters of palest green pendent cups. 2 ft. Any fertile soil, preferably shady. (See page 54.)

H. foetidus Handsome dark green divided leaves, below airy clusters of paler green flowers, each one a small perfect bell edged with maroon. Most striking, useful and easiest of helle-bores. Will grow anywhere, any soil, sun or shade. Evergreen. 18 in.

H. orientalis hybrids (Lenten rose) Varying in colour from blush white to deep purple-plum. Wide open, nodding flowers, often spotted inside with maroon, and with subtle green flushes both inside and out. Happy in any soil except bog, best in dappled or full shade. 18 in.

IRIS *foetidissima* Rich green evergreen leaves, thriving in any drained soil, including pure chalk. Flowers small, yellowish with purple veins. The autumn pods burst open displaying vivid orange seeds. 2 ft.

NEPETA *gigantea* (sage family; catmint) sun lovers, well-drained soil. Feathery masses of tiny greyish aromatic leaves and feathery flower spikes. 2½ ft.

PULMONARIA (borage family; lungwort) *angustifolia azurea* Creates the first splash of true blue in early spring. Ultra-marine-blue tubes are borne in clusters at the end of the stalks. There are soft rose and white varieties. All excellent as ground cover. 9 in.

SEDUM *spectabile* 'Autumn Joy' Sun-lovers, best in well-drained, poor soil. Flowers borne in large flat heads of rich salmon-bronze with tracings of emerald green. Greyish foliage.

TELLIMA Invaluable evergreen ground cover for sun or shade in any soil that does not dry out and is not boggy. *T. grandiflora*: a mat of rounded, hairy leaves up to 1 ft high, slowly spreading. Spikes of pale green, fringed bells appear in May. 2 ft.

Climbing plants to cover large banks or flat ground
CLEMATIS *montana*: See Climbers, page 70.

HYDRANGEA *petiolaris*: See Climbers, page 72.

LONICERA (honeysuckle) *japonica* 'Halliana' Evergreen, creamy yellow flowers July–October. Clip over hard in early March.

L. periclymenum ('Early Dutch' common honeysuckle) Creamy pink, very fragrant.

VITIS *coignetiae*: See Climbers, page 73.

Spreading Shrubs
The following shrubs spread over the soil, rooting as they go:

COTONEASTER *dammeri* Completely prostrate; red berries. 6 in. Increases indefinitely in sun or shade.

C. horizontalis Fish-bone like branches studded with scarlet berries in autumn, often remaining into winter. 4 ft by 12 ft.

C. microphyllus 'Cochleatus' Broader leaves than most of the family, large red berries. Dense 6 in ground cover.

C. 'Saldam' Arching habit. Narrow leaves, red berries. 3 ft by 10 ft.

HEDERA (ivy) All can be used, but the *Helix* varieties are excellent ground cover even in bone-dry soil and dense shade.

H. hibernica (Irish ivy) Dark green leaves with burnished tints in winter. Extremely rampant.

134   Sea buckthorn (*Hippophae rhamnoides*). *See page 149.*

JUNIPERUS (pine family) Spreading feathery shrubs. Limy and other soil, best in sun.

J. communis 'Hornibrookii' Dark green. 9 in.

J. conferta Fresh green spreading ground cover. Only for sheltered gardens.

J. horizontalis 'Douglassi' The growths turn violet-blue in winter. Valuable ground cover. 6 in. Spreading.

ROSA *paulii* Vigorous ground coverer. Procumbent, thorny stems arch over each other, making a dense low thicket, smothering all weeds. A gay sight when in flower with masses of wide, crinkled white blooms and golden stamens. Rich clover scent. 4 ft by 15 ft.

R. paulii 'Rosea'. Rather less vigorous than the white form; the flowers more beautiful than other single pink roses. The broad petals are like folded silk, a beautiful tone of pink; the yellow stamens surrounded by a clear white zone. Rich clove scent. 4 ft by 9 ft.

R. wichuriana A first-rate, completely prostrate evergreen trailer. The small dark green glossy leaves cover the ground, studded by the sprays of small, single, cream flowers in August. Dense growth for ground cover, pillar or wall. No pruning other than to keep control. Smells deliciously of green apples. Small oval hips.

R. 'Max Graf' This invaluable creeping rose roots as it grows and will eventually cover a large area with dense fresh greenery like that of a rambler. The single bright pink blooms are borne in clusters for a long period. Rich scent of green apples.

RUBUS *tricolor* (ornamental bramble) Glossy dark leaves cover trailing, furry brown stems. Dense and prolific ground cover for sheltered gardens, sun or shade. Grows 10 ft wide in a year.

SALIX *gillottii* (willow) Excellent quickly-spreading ground

136

cover. Small greyish leaves, yellow catkins in spring. Sun or part shade, 1 ft.

S. lanata 'Stuartii' Fine form, with fat, erect catkins appearing before the leaves which are large, rounded, woolly-grey. Any soil, sun or shade, 2 ft by 4 ft.

S. repens 'Argentea' Pretty form whose low, spreading branchlets are set with yellow catkins in spring, followed by small silver-grey leaves.

9 FOLIAGE PLANTS

The following list includes plants with grey, silver or glaucous foliage. (The term 'glaucous' describes leaves that are blue-green or blue-grey and covered by a 'bloom'.)

ACAENA *buchananii* Mats of grey-green leaves, with large green-spined burrs hiding beneath. 2 in. Splendid for growing between paving.

ACHILLEA (yarrow) In variety. Easy culture with attractive feathery foliage, silver, grey-green. Various heights.

ALYSSUM *montanum* Bright yellow flowers, grey foliage. 3 in.

ANAPHALIS *margaritacea* 'Pearly Everlasting' Grey leaves with heads of white flowers with pearly-white covering.

ARTEMISIA *absinthium* 'Lambrook Silver' An attractive silver form of our native wormwood. 3 ft.

BALLOTA *pseudodictamnus* Heart-shaped white, woolly leaves. Flowers white with purple spots. 2 ft.

CENTAUREA *pulcherrima* Deeply-cut silver foliage and bright rose-pink flowers. $2\frac{1}{2}$ ft.

CHRYSANTHEMUM *argenteum* Very attractive sub-shrubby plant with prostrate branches densely clothed with greyish white, finely cut leaves. 6 in.

C. densum amangum The finely cut leaves are bright silver-white.

138

The hosta family are grown primarily for their handsome foliage. (*H. sieboldiana*). See page 140.

C. praeteritum Grey-foliaged sub-shrub similar to *C. argenteum* but with leaflets even more finely divided, and arranged in herring-bone formation.

CONVOLVULUS *cneorum* Good rock garden shrub with silvery leaves and large pale pink and white, funnel-shaped flowers. $1\frac{1}{2}$ ft.

C. tenuissimus Finely-cut silver-grey foliage, and large bright pink flowers. A creeping plant. 6 in.

CYNARIA *scolymus* 'Glauca' (globe artichoke) One of our most ornamental plants. Magnificent glaucous foliage and large, blue thistle-like flowers. 5 ft.

ERYNGIUM *bourgatti* (sea holly) A dwarf species. The deeply-cut glaucous leaves are splashed with grey-white markings and have jagged edges. The stout stems have large blue thimble flowers. $1\frac{1}{2}$ ft. Thrives in light, well-drained soil.

EUPHORBIA (spurge) Many varieties.

HELIANTHEMUM (rock rose) Many varieties of silver and ever-grey-green leaved plants for dry, sunny positions, ranging in flower colour from orange, yellow or white, to rose, red and scarlet, double and single. 6 to 9 in.

HOSTA *sieboldiana* Very striking species with large, blue-green glaucous leaves. Flower pale lilac. 2 ft. Thrives in any soil which is not too dry and is of particular value for semi-shaded positions. (See page 139.)

KNIPHOFIA (red-hot-poker) Many varieties. Of great value for bold effect of sword-like evergreen leaves.
K. caulescens Flowers buff, changing to pale red. Glaucous yucca-like foliage.

LAVENDULA (lavender) Many varieties with silver-grey foliage and flower spikes ranging from deep violet to lilac-pink.

LEONTOPODIUM *alpinum* (edelweiss) Inconspicuous flowers surrounded by white woolly bracts. 6 in.

MACLEAYA *cordata* (plume poppy) Leaves are beautifully lobed, grey-green above and grey-white beneath. Spikes of numerous small buff or flesh-tinted starry flowers. 5 ft.

NEPETA *faassenii* (catmint) Its grey foliage, lavender-mauve flowers and obliging habit make it an invaluable edging plant. 1 ft.

ONOPORDUM *acanthium* (Scotch thistle) Strong-growing thistle, suitable for the border. Leaves ovate, grey-white. Flowers purple. 5 ft.

ONOSMA *albo-roseum* Grey hair leaves, arching sprays of white flowers changing to pink. 6 in.

PHILOMIS *viscosa* Handsome perennial resembling the shrubby Jerusalem sage. Leaves hoary, wrinkled, the basal ones large and heart-shaped. Flowers yellow, borne in conspicuous whorls in June. 3 to 5 ft.

ROMNEYA *coulteri* (tree poppy) Beautiful sea-green foliage and stems which reach a height of 4 ft or more. Flowers large, satiny white, with a mass of golden stamens.

RUTA *graveolens* 'Jackman's blue' (herb of grace) Long-cultivated evergreen herb with medicinal properties. The bright yellow flowers contrast with the striking blue foliage. Compact bushy habit. 2 ft.

SALVIA *argentea* The beauty of this plant lies in its large silvery-felted leaves. 2 ft.

SANTOLINA (lavender cotton) In variety.

STACHYS *lanata* 'Lavandulifolia' (lamb's tongue) A sub-shrubby plant, spreading by rhizomes, with narrow grey felted leaves.

(*Above*) Eryngium (*E. giganteum*). When dried, the Eryngium family make handsome winter decorations. The smaller *E. bourgatti* is also an attractive foliage plant. (*Opposite*) Garrya (*G. elliptica*). Again, popular with the flower arranger. *See pages 140 and 148.*

Flowers rose-purple, whorls. Should be given full sun and reasonable drainage. 1½ ft.

THALICTRUM *glaucum* (meadow rue) A family distinguished by its delicate foliage, comparable with that of the maidenhair fern. Glaucous foliage, pale yellow flowers. 5 ft.

THYMUS *pseudolanuginosus* (thyme) A hairy, prostrate plant, forming grey mats. The reluctant flowers are pink. ½ in.

VERBASCUM 'Broussa' Handsome plants apt to turn up in unexpected places from self-sown seed. The tall spikes remain colourful from early summer onwards. Flowers bright yellow, leaves large, covered with white down. 6 ft.

VERONICA (speedwell) In variety.

Plants for flower arranging
The plants in the following list have flowers or foliage of special interest to the arranger.

Abutilon
Acanthus mollis 'Lactifolius'
A. spinosus
Acer (Japanese maples)
Achillea, various
Agapanthus, various
Alchemilla mollis
Amelanchier
Astrantia, various
Berberis, various
Buddleia fallowiana
Callicarpa giraldiana
    (berry)
Carex pendula 'Sedge'
Chimonanthus.
Cornus alba varieties
C. stolonifera
Cotoneaster franchetti (berry)

C. salicifolius floccosus (berry)
Corylopsis spicata
Cytisus
Deutzia
Dierama pulcherrima
Echinops, various
Elaeagnus
Epimedium, various
Eremurus, various
Erica (some varieties)
Eryngium, various (See page 142.)
Euphorbia characias
E. wulfenii
Forsythia
Fuchsia
Garrya
Grasses, various
Hamamelis

144

Kniphofia, various
Hosta, various
Hydrangea
Hypericum 'Elstead' (berry)
Jasminum polyanthum
Lavandula liatris 'Pycnostachya'
Liatris spicata
Linaria purpurea
L. p. 'Canon J. Went'
Lomatia
Lonicera
Luzula nivea
Macleaya cordata
Mahonia japonica
Morina longifolia
Peltiphyllum peltatum
Pernettya (berry)
Philadelphus

Physalis franchetii
Pieris
Polygonatum hybridum
P. amplexicaule, and varieties
P. bistro 'Superbum'
Prunus triloba
Rhus cotinus 'Foliis purpureis'
Rose species, in variety
Sanguisorba, various
Schizostylis coccinea, various
Sisyrinchium striatum
Spartium
Spiraea, various
Stachys lanata
Symphoricarpus (berry)
Symplocos paniculatus (berry)
Verbena bonariensis
Weigela

10 SEASIDE PLANTING

The greatest difficulty, particularly on the cold east coast, is the dry, parching wind generally experienced in spring and early summer, although the actual force of the wind is probably less than on the west coast, where the climate is warmer and damper.

The salt-laden winds may cause browning of evergreens but there is the advantage that severe frosts seldom occur near the sea. This is the reason why it is possible to grow near the sea many plants which, if planted inland, would need a cool greenhouse in winter.

Much time and trouble will be saved if you can put up some form of temporary windguard at planting time. It is surprising how even a small-meshed fence of wire or plastic netting will filter the wind, while if larger meshed netting is threaded with sprigs of conifers and evergreens, then even more protection will be given. Wattle hurdles and the innumerable other screens made of interwoven material are all suitable for the purpose, providing they are well anchored and buttressed.

Of the conifers, *Cupressocyparis leylandii* is in the front rank of defences due to its amazing tolerance of salt-laden winds, its rapid, dense growth and pleasing foliage. *Cupressus macrocarpa*, one of the parents of the above, is far better near the sea than inland.

The pines provide excellent hedges and screens and are by no means slow growing. All are suitable as first rank defences except for the Scots pine, which does better in the second row.

The Lombardy poplar is a good seaside subject, as is the

silver poplar, *P. alba*, which has dark green leaves with white felt underneath; also *P. eugenii* which is very fast growing.

Other front liners include *Acer pseudoplatanus*, sycamore, *Crataegus*, thorn, *Salix*, willow, *Sorbus*, mountain ash, *Quercus ilex*, evergreen or holm oak and *Ulmus*, elm.

Some trees for the second line include *Acer plantanoides*, Norway maple, *Alnus glautinosa*, alder, *Betula*, birch and *Fagus*, beech.

Planting
Ground should be well prepared, with plenty of sedge peat and humus well watered in at planting time, especially where the soil is sandy. The plants should not have to fight against adverse conditions in the soil as well as above it.

Nothing is gained by planting the largest specimens you can buy. Like us, the older we are the less we care to be transplanted. Younger, and less expensive plants, quickly outstrip them in a few years.

Trees and shrubs should be most firmly staked, and plantings should be much closer than recommended for inland. The shoulder-to-shoulder method appears to keep the plants going, and the wind out.

Trees and shrubs suitable for coastal areas

ABELIA

ABUTILON

ARBUTUS *unedo* (strawberry tree; see page 112)

BERBERIS In variety; good shrubs for first line of defence of windswept sites.

BUDDLEIA *davidii* varieties. Very quick effect.

BUPLEURUM *fruticosum* Evergreen shrub with umbels of yellow flowers.

CARYOPTERIS Small shrub for full sun. Clip over in spring like lavender.

CHOISYA *ternata* (Mexican orange blossom) Needs shelter.

147

CISTUS (rock rose) In variety.

COLUTEA *arborescens* (bladder senna) Quick effect on poor soil in hot, dry sites. Attractive pinnate foliage. First line of defence shrub.

CONVOLVULUS *cneorum* A mass of silvery, silky leaves covered with silky white trumpets after pink buds.

COTONEASTER

CRATAEGUS (hawthorn) Many varieties; useful as first line of defence.

CUPRESSUS *macrocarpa* and 'Lutea'. Green and gold conifers

CYTISUS (broom)

ELAEAGNUS *ebbingei* Rapid-growing vigorous evergreen shrub. Beautiful olive-green, broad, glossy leaves, silvered beneath. Young leaves also silvery. Tiny creamy bells in autumn with rich fragrance. Use as a specimen, as background or informal hedge. Considered the most important evergreen to be introduced for many years.

ESCALLONIA In variety. (See page 109.)

EUCALYPTUS *gunnii*

EUONYMUS *japonica* (evergreen spindle tree) Densely leafy, bushy shrubs with leathery polished green leaves. Any position. 5 by 6 ft, for front line of defence.

FAGUS (beech)

FATSIA

FORSYTHIA

FRAXINUS *excelsior* (common ash)

FUCHSIA In variety.

GARRYA *elliptica* Fascinating quick-growing evergreen with long, dangling, grey-green, silky catkins in January–February. (See page 143.)

GRISELINIA *littoralis* A golden evergreen shrub, 10 by 6 ft which

148

can stand really salt-laden winds. Chalk-tolerant but dislikes heavy clays.

HEBE *Veronica, H. salicifolia*; *H. speciosa* varieties; *H. traversii*. Evergreen shrubs for front line of defence.

HEDERA (ivy)

HIBISCUS (tree hollyhock) Needs good soil and full sun. (See page 115.)

HIPPOPHAE *rhamnoides* (sea buckthorn) Masses of translucent orange berries appear against narrow leaves with silver undersides. Very striking. Thrives on arid soils. Plant in groups of both sexes. (See page 135.)

HORNBEAM

HYDRANGEA *hortensis* In variety. *H. paniculata*; *H.* 'Grandiflora'.

HYPERICUMS

ILEX (holly) In variety.

KERRIA Close clumps of slender green stems in winter. Dainty leaves and buttercup yellow flowers, 4–5 ft.

LABURNUM

LAVENDER In variety

LIGUSTRUM (privet)

LONICERA *nitida* (honeysuckle) Tiny dark evergreen leaves, rapidly reaching 3–4 ft.

MAHONIA In variety.

OLEARIA *haastii* Box-like evergreen leaves over a dense bush; smothered with fragrant white daisy flowers. 5 by 5 ft. Front liners. *O. macrodonta* Grey downy 'Holly' leaves. Mass of white flowers July–August. 7 by 6 ft. Takes seaside gales on the chin.

OSMANTHUS Evergreen shrubs valued for their exquisitely fragrant white tubular flowers. Need wall protection in cold areas to be at their best.

PERNETTYA Superb berrying evergreens. Shining round berries lasting through the winter and unaffected by the weather. Dense thickets of wiry stems which reach 3 ft and spread indefinitely. One male and three female plants are needed to produce berries. Must have an acid, lime-free soil.

PEROVSKIA (Russian sage) Outstanding late summer shrub. Deep blue flower spikes. The whole plant shrouded in silvery white down except the flowers. 3 by 2 ft.

PHILADELPHUS (mock orange) Grows even in the poorest soils if mulched with manure.

PHLOMIS *fruticosa* (Jerusalem sage) Semi-evergreen, with quaint bright yellow stalkless flowers at the tips of the shoots, June–July. 3 by 4 ft. Good for sunny bank, any soil.

PINUS *radiata* (Monterey pine); *P. sylvestris* (Scots pine); *P. austriaca* (Austrian pine).

POPULUS *alba* (white poplar)

POTENTILLA In variety.

PRUNUS *pissardu* (purple leaf plum); *P. cerasifera* (cherry plum) varieties; *P. laurocerasus* (common laurel).

PYRACANTHA

RHUS (sumach)

RIBES (flowering currant)

ROMNEYA (tree poppy)

ROSA *rugosa* and other strong-growing roses.

ROSMARINUS (rosemary)

SALIX (willow)

SAMBUCUS (elder) In variety. Front line defence.

SANTOLINA

SENECIO In variety. *S. laxifolius*, front line defence.

SKIMMIA In variety.

150

SORBUS *aria* (whitebeam) *S. intermedia* (Swedish whitebeam)

SPARTICUM *junceum* (Spanish broom) Thrives on chalk or sand, full sun. Front line defence.

SPIRAEA

SYMPHORICARPUS (snowberry) In variety. Front line defence.

TAMARISK In variety. Fine feathery foliage and flowers resistant to sea winds. All are quick growing and graceful. Thrive in all but the heaviest soils. Full sun. Front line defence.

ULEX (double-flowered gorse) A blaze of golden yellow fragrant flowers April–May but seldom without flower. Best on dry soil. Tidier than common gorse. 6 by 5 ft.

VIBURNUM *tinum* One of the few winter flowering evergreens and the easiest to grow. They thrive in sun or shade.

WEIGELA

YUCCA *filamentosa* (Adam's needle).

11 SPECIAL PURPOSE PLANTS

There are always odd spots in the garden where it is difficult to grow things. Some never see the sun; others too much of it, so I have selected a number of plants that will thrive in these surroundings, and others that will take kindly to particular soil conditions.

Sometimes there are freak conditions to contend with, such as a garden in an alkaline area having a seam of acid soil running through it, where rhodendrons and azaleas thrive . . . the only examples for miles around. This can happen, so make sure that you know *all* of your garden and its peculiarities.

Sunless positions

Acer (Japanese varieties)
Acer (Snake Bark varieties)
Aucuba japonica
Avena
Azalea pontica
Berberis
Buxus (box)
Camellia
Chaenomeles (ornamental quince)
Choisya
Cornus alba varieties
Cotoneaster (low-growing varieties)
Daphne

Euonymus radicans
Fatsia
Festuca
Garrya
Gaultheria
Hedera (ivy)
Hydrangea
Hypericum calycinum
Ilex (holly; not golden varieties)
Jasmine
Kerria
Laurel
Leycesteria
Ligustrum (privet)

Lonicera (honeysuckle)
Mahonia aquifolium
Molina
Olearia haastii
Osmanthus
Osmarea
Pachysandra
Pennisetum
Pernettya
Phillyrea
Pyracantha
Ribes (flowering currant)
Rhododendron (in variety,
    including azaleas)
Rubus
Ruscus
Sambucus
Sarcococca
Skimmia
Spiraea ('Anthony Waterer')
S. ariaefolia
Stripa
Symphoricarpus
Viburnum (winter flowering
    varieties)
Vinca

Hot dry sites

In the following list, those plants which thrive on banks are
marked with an asterisk.

Artemisia abrotanum
Atriplex
Berberis*
Box
Caryopteris
Chaenomeles (flowering
    quince)
Cistus (rock rose)*
Colutea*
Cortaderia
Cotoneaster* (low varieties)
Cytisus (broom)*
Erica
Euonymus radicans 'Variegata'
Genista*
Hebe
Hedera*
Hedysarum
Helichrysum (everlasting)
Hippophae (sea buckthorn)
Hypericum*
Indigofera
Juniperus (low varieties)
Lavandula (lavender)
Olearia
Perovskia
Phlomis
Potentilla
Rhus cotinus
Robinia
Rosa spinosissima varieties
Rosemary
Rubus
Santolina*
Senecio
Spartium*
Spiraea
Tamarix
Ulex (gorse)*
Veronica
Vinca*
Yucca

Peat loving plants

The following plants dislike chalk and limestone soils:

Azaleas
Bruckenthalia
Camellia
Conifer (some varieties)
Corylopsis
Daboecia
Enkianthus
Erica (some varieties)

Fothergilla
Gaultheria
Malmia
Magnolia (some varieties)
Pernettya
Pieris
Rhododendron

For chalk and lime soils

Abelia
Acer (except *A. Japonicum* and *A. palmatum* varieties)
Aucuba
Azara
Barberia
Buddleia
Cercis
Chaenomeles (flowering quince)
Chimonanthus (See page 62)
Choisya
Cistus (rock rose)
Clematis
Clerodendron
Cornus
Cotoneaster
Crataegus
Cytisus battandieri (Moroccan broom, see page 63)
Daphne
Deutzia
Diervilla
Escallonia (See page 109)

Euonymus europaeus
Forsythia
Hibiscus
Hypericum
Ilex (holly)
Laurel
Ligustrum (privet)
Lilac (syringa)
Magnolia kobus
Malus (flowering crab)
Paeonia delavayi
Philadelphus
Pittosporum
Potentilla
Prunus (all sections)
Pyracantha
Rhus (sumach)
Ribes (flowering currant)
Rubus
Senecio
Spiraea
Symphoricarpus
Syringa (lilac)
Viburnum

154

INDEX

Both Latin and common names, where applicable, are included in this index. Figures in bold type refer to illustrations.

155